Between stone and steel

OrangeBooks Publication

1st Floor, Rajhans Arcade, Mall Road, Kohka, Bhilai, Chhattisgarh 490020
Website: **www.orangebooks.in**

First Edition, 2026

ISBN: 978-93-7426-993-0

BETWEEN STONE AND STEEL

ENGINEERS JOURNEY OF ENDURANCE

SHAHBAZ KHAN

OrangeBooks Publication
www.orangebooks.in

BETWEEN STONE AND STEEL

ENGINEERS JOURNEY OF ENDURANCE

SHAHBAZ KHAN

OrangeBooks Publication
www.orangebooks.in

Preface

When a fresh graduate steps into the manufacturing industry, they enter with boundless energy, enthusiasm, and determination to prove themselves. They willingly put in long hours, stretch beyond schedules, and give more than what is asked of them. From day one, they are told the standard rule, "eight hours of work, one weekly off," yet in practice, they rarely claim it. Instead, they pour themselves into work, often at the cost of their personal life, because they want to impress superiors and live up to expectations.

I know this because I lived it.

I am Shahbaz Khan, and I began my journey in one of the best cement industries. I was naive, nervous, and insecure. My knowledge was limited, my frame was thin, and behind my -2 powered spectacles were eyes filled with both fear and ambition. My palms sweated as I tried to keep up, desperate to satisfy my bosses.

In that struggle, I lost my balance of life. Washing clothes was a luxury. Self-care was non-existent. Many days, meals were skipped. Nights shrank into 3–4 hours of broken sleep. Sometimes I wore the same clothes for 3–4 days, until sweat left salt stains across my pants and shirt. The sun burned my skin, lips cracked dry, and my spectacles often fogged with grime I didn't have time to clean. In between long shifts, I thought about my college loans, my siblings' marriages, my parents' needs, all while searching for a water cooler to quench a thirst that never ended. Life as a novice felt like working inside a mine. Dark, consuming and suffocating.

I still remember what it meant to be called to the plant when a machine broke down. The call narrowed our lives instantly. Everything else receded. Hours stretched into long, unbroken stretches of work. Meals were postponed. Rest disappeared. The skin carried coal and limestone dust for days. Fatigue was worn like part of the uniform. In those moments, our attention was focused on only a few things: arranging spares, finding lifting equipment, gathering the right people and restoring movement. Around us, pressure always accumulated steadily. Calls arrived one after another, each repeating the same expectation, to start the machine at the earliest. Even when the plant fell silent at night, our minds hummed the constant rhythm of the plant we had gotten so used.

Working alongside us were veterans shaped by a different era. Some relied entirely on pocket diaries rather than screens, carrying their knowledge in handwritten notes accumulated over decades. That diary carried their identity, confidence and relevance in a system that was slowly changing around them. Watching them taught me that experience can be both a source of strength and a place of quiet vulnerability.

Between crises, brief pauses appeared in unlikely places. A small tea hut near the site offered moments of relief. Those pauses mattered more than they appeared to at the time. They restored perspective, however briefly, in an environment that rewarded endurance more than reflection.

Above all, I observed how responsibility expressed itself differently across roles. Senior leaders spoke of long hours and past struggles, while their days followed rhythms that allowed distance from the shop floor. For those of us closer to the machines, survival demanded far longer stretches of attention and effort. The contrast was instructive. It revealed how systems distribute pressure unevenly, and how leadership is experienced very differently depending on where one stands.

These early years shaped my understanding of work, leadership and resilience. They taught me that industries run on more than equipment and processes. This book grows out of those observations. It reflects on what professional life demands, what it quietly takes away, and what must be consciously rebuilt to sustain both performance and well-being over time.

The pages that follow do not celebrate exhaustion. They attempt to understand it and to ask what kind of leadership becomes possible once reflection replaces reaction. This contrast, between the naive youth sacrificing life to growing as a impactful leader, defines the essence of manufacturing culture. This book is born from that tension. It is not just a study of work-life balance; it is a lived account of imbalance, of sacrifice, of resistance, and of the urgent need for change. It is my call for a culture where efficiency embraces technology, where seniors guide without stifling, and where young professionals can grow without losing themselves.

Work must never come at the expense of living. Work-life balance is not a luxury; it is a way of living.

Acknowledgement

No book is written alone; though many are typed in solitude. This one is no exception. What follows is not merely a formal courtesy, but an honest recognition of the many visible and invisible forces that shaped the thinking behind these pages. This book has been assembled from success, failures, conversations, silences and the steady presence of people who never asked to be acknowledged, but deserve it most.

First and always, my deepest gratitude belongs to my family. They bore the unseen costs of this work with a grace that words struggle to honour. They endured late evenings that quietly slipped into early mornings and conversations gently paused mid-sentence as thoughts took over me many a times. They understood my peculiar absence of being physically present yet mentally elsewhere and never mistook it for indifference. Their patience turned these small disappearances into a form of grace that only they could manifest. Their constant support kept me deeply grounded and grateful. In moments of doubt, their belief in me remained steady and kept me steadily moving forward. Every demanding chapter in my professional life was made possible by the emotional stability they provided. This book rests, quite literally, on that foundation.

I owe an enduring debt to the colleagues, mentors and teams with whom I have worked across manufacturing floors, project rooms, crisis meetings and improvement reviews. Engineers, technicians, operators, supervisors, managers and leaders, each played a significant role in shaping how I think about responsibility and leadership. They taught me lessons no textbook could; that a process is only as strong as the people who run it, that competence reveals itself under pressure and that trust is built not through authority but through consistency. Every breakdown restored, every target missed, every uncomfortable conversation and every quiet success refined my understanding of what leadership truly demands. These pages are filled with their echoes.

I am deeply thankful to the organizations and professional ecosystems that allowed me not just to succeed, but to continuously learn from it. They entrusted me with complex systems, tight deadlines, high-stakes decisions and the responsibility to lead people through uncertainty. They offered me perspective which I consider far more valuable than success. Daily exposure to operational realities grounded the thinking behind this book. Continuous improvement cultures sharpened its discipline and rigor. Human dynamics under pressure gave it depth and honesty. Together, these experiences form the intellectual spine of this book. I learned that transformation is hardly ever tidy and growth almost always begins with discomfort. I remain grateful for these humbling and empowering opportunities.

I also acknowledge the thinkers, authors, teachers and quiet intellectual companions whose ideas challenged and sharpened my own. Some I met through books, some through lectures and some through insights passed casually in conversation. Their influence has orientated me towards systems thinking, resilience, humility and long-term clarity. If this book carries any intellectual rigor, it is because I stood on the shoulders of those who thought deeply before me. To those who challenged me, sometimes directly and sometimes unintentionally, thank you. You questioned my assumptions, tested my patience and exposed the limits of my thinking. In moments of resistance, you forced me to look harder and grow stronger.

Finally, I thank you. The reader. Choosing to engage with a book is an act of trust and time investment, both of which are increasingly scarce. If these pages help you pause before reacting, think more clearly under pressure, lead with greater calm or feel less alone in the complications of responsibility, then this work has fulfilled its intent. If it helps you ask better questions of yourself, your teams or your systems, then it has done meaningful work.

This acknowledgement, like the book itself, is a reminder that growth is never linear, leadership is never solitary and meaningful work is never the result of individual brilliance alone. It is built gradually, one deliberate step at a time. Each lesson learned adds a small but lasting layer. Service shapes it by shifting focus away from self and toward responsibility. Perseverance holds everything together when progress feels invisible. I thank you for your willingness to share that weight by choosing to pick this book up.

With deepest gratitude and respect,

~Shahbaz Khan

Contents

Chapter 1
Probation Confirmation Period

It was August 2009. I had just graduated, armed with optimism and an off-campus placement letter that felt like a golden ticket. My parents saw it as the family's first real step toward security. I saw it as the opening line of a legend I was eager to write. But legends, I would soon learn, began with chaos. Like riding the Force Toofan that was carrying me to the plant hostel. It looked harmless enough from the outside. But inside, it was a human puzzle; twenty people crammed into a nine-seater, bags piled high, elbows in ribs, and somewhere near the gearbox, a baby crying as if protesting the injustice of engineering. The driver treated the steering wheel like a percussion instrument, slapping clutch and brake in erratic rhythm. Every pothole felt like a quality-check test for my spine.

After three long hours of jolts and sweat, we finally reached the gate. My shirt clung to me like a second skin. A giant board announced the company name, factory, in bold letters, invoking a mix of pride and fear in me. Beneath it, in smaller print, was the motto: Safety First. I had no idea then that, in this world, safety would often come last.

The hostel stood on a barren stretch of land, half hidden behind rows of neem trees. The warden handed me a key labelled Room 107. Inside were four cots arranged side by side, one ancient ceiling fan. In front of the beds stood a long metal almirah fitted with crezenda-style shelves and four drawers, one for each occupant. Space was a luxury we didn't have, so our belongings lived in layers. The bathroom situation was its own daily battle. One common toilet served nearly a dozen rooms, at least twenty men competing for a few minutes of running water. Mornings almost always began with the sound of knocking, pleading, and arguments outside the washroom door. It was the raw, unfiltered beginning of my life as a plant engineer.

My roommates arrived one by one. Two Bengalis, Debjyoti and Saurav Sen, and a Tamilian named N Selvan. The room smelled like a spice box from my mother's kitchen. Amid the medley of accents, there pulsed an infinite energy of new beginnings. That first night, we bonded over shared snacks, laughter, and nervous dreams of the plant. I slept light. Somewhere in the distance, I could hear the hum of a kiln.

Morning began before sunrise. The bus to the plant honked precisely at 7:15 a.m. By 8:30 we were inside the gate, standing awkwardly with files and ID card. Mr. Arvind, our manager, arrived at 9:00 a.m. He was a tall man with a proudly curled moustache and an aura that mixed discipline with theatre. He barely looked up from his register when he said, "Shahbaz Khan, you join the Raw Mill project." And just like that, my training began. There was no orientation, no warm handshake of introduction, no mentor to ease me in. With no office space available, we hauled an old metal container onto the site, wiped off dust, and christened it our "office." Inside, we placed a single stool and a rickety table that wobbled with every movement. That container became everything, our control room, job allocation centre and tea corner.

Mr. Manish, the millwright fitter, was the first to take me around. His palms were as rough as sandpaper, his nails rimmed with grease, and his humour was drier than cement in summer. He had the easy confidence of a man who could fix a machine by instinct alone. As we walked through the roaring shop floor, he gestured toward the towering structures and said, half in jest and half in truth, "Get to know these machines as well as you can, Shahbaz. They'll be your only love here." I laughed nervously, not realizing then how right he was.

The Raw Mill looked enormous; steel beams stretching skyward, conveyors twisting like serpents, and dust dancing in every sunbeam. The roar of the fan drowned all other sounds; even thoughts seemed to be silenced. My German colleague, Mr. Gerd, frowned each time someone took out a phone. "Discipline!" he often barked.

Within hours, my neat white helmet had turned grey. Sweat carved channels down my face. I tried to remember each motor's rating, every valve's name, each safety tag's colour code, but by noon my head felt like an overloaded circuit. Still, there was thrill. I was touching the heartbeat of industry. The hum of the mill, the rhythm of conveyors, the occasional thud of clinker falling, they became my music. I thought to myself: *This is where engineers are forged.* Back in the container office, I buried myself in equipment manuals. Hydraulic circuits looked like alien maps. Flow diagrams ran into each other like spaghetti. When I asked questions, half were answered with a shrug, half with a joke. Evening was even more mechanical. After the bus ride back, I queued for dinner at *Annapurna Mess*—rice, dal, and endless talk about machine failures. By 9:00 p.m. I found myself in bed, exhausted but restless. The thin mattress was nowhere near comfortable.

The next morning I discovered the rigid hierarchy in the plant. Veterans guarded their wisdom like classified data. I watched seniors write everything in pocket diaries. Mr. Manohar, the diary-king as we called him, believed Microsoft Excel was witchcraft. Once he lost his diary and declared half the plant paralyzed until it was found. Meanwhile, we juniors lived on adrenaline and unpaid overtime. "Eight-hour shift" was fiction. Twelve, sometimes sixteen hours were normal. Reporting late by ten minutes meant a scolding; working late by four hours meant "dedication." My body

adjusted, reluctantly. Meals skipped, clothes unwashed, skin tanned beyond recognition. But inside all that fatigue was a spark, the urge to prove that I belonged among giants of machinery.

Amid everything, our biggest stress-buster was the tea hut. It stood just outside the main gate, a small bamboo shack with a tin roof that clattered in the wind and a coal stove that never rested. The smell of strong tea and burnt coal, somehow, brought peace amid all the work chaos. Whenever fatigue clouded my head or tension from the control room followed me outside, I'd find myself there instinctively. The tea-seller was an old man with cracked hands and an easy smile. We sat on a wooden plank balanced over paint tins, pouring tea into our mouths and letting the day's frustration pour right out with it.

Three weeks in, it happened. A hydraulic leak at the Raw Mill brought production to a standstill. My heart pounded; adrenaline replaced fear. Everyone shouted orders. I tried to trace the leak, slipping on oil, fingers trembling. Mr. Manish barked instructions while Mr. Gerd hovered, muttering "Schnell! Schnell!" We worked twelve hours straight, drenched in oil, until the last fitting tightened and the mill roared back. The relief was electric.

As days turned into months, the excitement began to dull. By now, the plant had swallowed me whole. The days started blending into each other. The same bus horn. The same clatter of canteen plates. The same dust settling on helmets. I had stopped counting hours. Shift changes meant nothing when the phone could ring at any moment: "Shahbaz, breakdown in Raw Mill. Come fast." Fast became the only speed I knew. There was no schedule. Lunch breaks dissolved into tea breaks; tea breaks dissolved into missed meals. Once, while tracing a motor fault, I realized it was 11 p.m. and I hadn't eaten since breakfast. I poured tea into my mouth like fuel into a machine and went back to work. I told myself it was temporary, just until my probation is complete. But "temporary" stretched into months.

The effects of overtime followed soon. It all began subtly; persistent headaches and mild dizziness. I ignored it, thinking dehydration was just part of the deal. Then came a stabbing pain in my lower back, sharp enough to make me wince while tightening a flange bolt. The company doctor diagnosed it: dehydration-induced kidney stones. One in

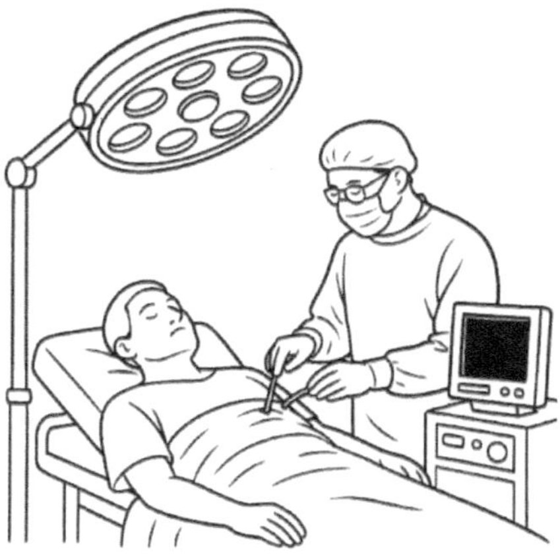

the left ureter—10 mm. Another in the right kidney—5

mm. A week later I was on an operating table under harsh fluorescent lights, anesthetized and humbled. I remember the smell of antiseptic filled the corridor as nurses wheeled me toward the operation theatre. The ceiling lights were blindingly white. I lay on the narrow table, heart pounding, watching masked faces move around me with mechanical precision. A nurse tied a band around my arm to raise a vein. I felt the quick sting of one injection, then another and then something stronger that sent a faint warmth racing up my hand. My pulse echoed in my ears. The anesthetist appeared beside me, voice calm and distant. "You'll feel a little cold now," he said, pressing the syringe into the line. He was right. A chill spread through my veins, then a heavy stillness. Sounds began to blur. I could sense movement, voices muffled behind masks, the hum of machines, and the rhythm of metallic tools touching the metallic trays. Someone adjusted a strap on my wrist. I remember the ceiling lights multiplying, sliding out of focus and then shrinking to a single, glowing point. For a brief moment, I drifted somewhere between waking and sleep. I wasn't sure if I was dreaming or hearing real voices. A doctor giving instructions, the faint beeping of a monitor, the smell of spirit and steel. My body felt far away. When I opened my eyes again, the lights were softer. A nurse whispered that everything had gone well and that a stent had been placed in my kidney and ureter to help pass the fragments. I wanted to feel the relief, but my throbbing temples and bandaged-abdomen forbade me to feel anything but pain. I was discharged the next day, and by the following morning, I was already back at the office. The post-surgery pain was constant. But two days later, even in that condition I was sent to Madhya Pradesh and Andhra Pradesh for upskilling.

My senior, Mr. Arvind, started trusting me completely. That should have been a compliment, but in the plant dictionary, trust meant availability 24x7. If the Raw Mill tripped, call Shahbaz. If Coal Mill stalled, call Shahbaz. If the Pyro line coughed, Cement Mill sneezed, or RMCH gasped, call Shahbaz. I became the unofficial helpline of the plant. It felt good, at first. Recognition is certainly addictive. Each “Good job” felt like an award. But underneath, exhaustion was quietly collecting interest. My phone was my leash. I kept it beside my plate during dinner, beside my pillow during sleep, beside my mat during prayers. The moment it buzzed, my pulse jumped. Pavlov’s dog had nothing on me. I said yes to everything. Yes to weekend shifts. Yes to budget files on Sundays. Yes to late-night inspections and early-morning reviews. The irony was bitter, while I helped the plant run smoothly, my own life was breaking down.

A few weeks later, HR called me in. I stood before the manager, still wearing my dusty uniform. He handed me a folder with the company logo. “Congratulations, Shahbaz. Your probation is cleared.” Back in the hostel, I shared sweets with my roommates. They clapped, cheered, and teased. “Now maybe you’ll finally wash your bedsheet!” Debjyoti said. I laughed. Maybe tomorrow, I thought.

Soon after confirmation, came promotion. My hard work was paying off. But with recognition came responsibility, and with responsibility came pressure that made the earlier days look like warm-up laps. The bosses trusted me with new projects, new people, new budgets. I was proud, but my body was rebelling. My pulse raced even when sitting still. Nights were restless, mornings mechanical. I knew every vibration of the Raw Mill, every hum of a healthy bearing, every sigh of a tired motor. My mind had started syncing with machines; I could almost sense an abnormal noise before it began. That intuitive bond made me efficient, but also dangerously comfortable. I had become the man who could fix anything except himself. One night, as I lay on my bed staring at the ceiling fan, I found myself wondering how it managed to spin tirelessly, day after day, without ever losing balance. I knew the answer, I realized. It was lubrication and rest. And here I was, grinding through the friction of work without ever switching myself off. I was worried I would lose balance.

I suppressed my emotions and agreed to every demand at the plant, sacrificing my own time and well-being. Family moments began slipping away like sand through clenched fingers. My father would call in the evenings, asking softly if I had eaten, and I'd reply half-distracted, "Yes, yes, I'll call later," though I rarely did. My mother's voice, once my daily comfort, became a sound I often postponed. Even her warmth had to wait for a free slot on my schedule. One evening, she called while I was still at the plant. I remember standing near the Raw Mill, helmet tucked under my arm, machinery rumbling in the background.

"Beta," she said, "your cousin Nida's wedding is next month. Everyone is asking if you'll come." For a moment I said nothing. My mind immediately began calculating shifts, project deadlines, pending reports. "Ammi, I don't think I can," I finally said, raising my voice over the roar of the fan. "You can't take even two days?" she asked gently, though I could hear the disappointment hiding behind her calm. "Not now. There's too much happening here. Maybe next time." There was a long pause. Then she sighed. She hesitated before replying, "Okay… take care of yourself, Shahbaz." The line went silent, but her unspoken sadness stayed with me long after.

Friends too had stopped asking after a while. The first few invitations came with excitement, birthdays, cricket matches, a weekend movie. I turned them down with polite excuses. "Next time," I'd say, until "next time" became a polite version of "never." Sometimes, on the bus ride back from the plant, I'd look out the window and see families sitting outside their quarters, children chasing each other, fathers sipping tea. I was twenty-three, yet already living like a man twice my age.

Disciplined, yes, but detached from the small, colourful chaos of youth.

Still, I convinced myself this was dedication. This was how legends were built. I told myself I was sculpting a career, not losing a life. “This is the time to push,” I’d whisper, almost like a prayer. “Work now, live later.” And so, I did, unaware that “later” was quietly slipping away with every call I declined.

Then on one Friday night, Debjyoti declared “Enough! We’re going to the city tomorrow.”

I looked up, startled. “City? What for?”

He grinned. “Movie. Shopping. Proper food. Maybe even a massage.”

I laughed, tired. “You go,” I said. “I can’t.”

Saurav leaned forward, waving his spoon like a general commanding an army. “If you can manage the Raw Mill, you can manage one day off. The world won’t stop spinning without you.”

“Tell that to Mr. Arvind,” I said, half joking, half terrified.

They didn’t laugh. They just stared at me, and in their silence I heard something truer than any advice, “*you’re losing yourself.*”

That night, while they packed their bags with casual joy, I sat staring at my phone. Asking for leave felt harder than facing a breakdown at the mill. Every time I imagined the conversation, my chest tightened. Three times I rehearsed my words: “Sir, may I take a day’s leave tomorrow?” and each time, I chickened out. When I finally dialed Mr. Arvind’s number, my palms were sweating.

The ring felt eternal. “Yes?” His voice was calm, distant, like always.

“Sir, I… I was thinking of taking a day’s leave tomorrow. Just for one day.”

A long pause. My throat went dry. Then, simply: “Okay, Shahbaz.”

I blinked. “Sir?”

“I said okay. Take care.” And he hung up.

I stared at the phone in disbelief. Why did it feel like I was being left on parole?!

The next morning, we packed into my red Nano. Seven of us. Three engineers, two technicians, and a couple of interns. The engine groaned under the weight, but we didn’t care. Windows rolled down, music loud, laughter louder. The highway stretched. On both sides, the landscape shifted from the industrial grey of the plant to open fields dotted with trees and grazing cattle. With every kilometer, the dust of the factory seemed to fall off our shoulders. We reached the city as if in no time and parked near a shopping complex that looked unreal in its brightness. We walked in like explorers entering a new civilization. The smell of popcorn and perfume hit us at once.

"Man, this feels like another planet," Saurav said, spinning slowly with his arms wide.

For the first time in months, I wasn't carrying a helmet or a toolkit. I wasn't worrying about vibration readings or oil leaks. We watched a movie, something loud and ridiculous, but I laughed so hard my stomach hurt. Then we went shopping. I bought two shirts, one blue, one white, more out of ritual than necessity. They still smelled faintly of the store when I unpacked them later, a reminder that I could still enjoy small luxuries. Lunch was biryani, proper biryani, not the mess version that looked like boiled rice with stage fright. We ate until our stomachs protested and then ordered desserts just because we could. Someone cracked a joke about calorific shutdowns, and the table burst into laughter. It felt strange at first, laughing without guilt. For months, my laughter had been reserved for sarcasm during breakdowns or quick chuckles between shifts. But this… this was real. It echoed from somewhere deeper.

After lunch, Debjyoti suggested we go to a spa. I almost refused. "Spa? We're engineers, not CEOs."

"Exactly," he said. "We need it more than they do."

So we went. The air smelled of lemongrass. A stranger asked me to lie down and began pressing the knots out of my shoulders. My muscles resisted at first, stiff and suspicious, but slowly they began to soften.

With each press, I felt something unclench, a muscle in my body, a neuron in my brain. For the first time in months, I wasn't bracing for a phone call, a machine breakdown, or a scolding. The silence felt soothing. I caught my reflection in the mirror across the room, face relaxed, a faint smile curling at the corners. I barely recognized that man.

That night, we stayed in a small hotel. The water was hot, the bed soft and the only hum I heard was from the air conditioner. Standing before the mirror, I looked at myself long and hard. The dark circles were still there, the tan lines still sharp, but behind them, I saw traces of something I had almost forgotten. I was alive.

The next morning, as we drove back, the road felt even shorter. The laughter was quieter now, more thoughtful. The city was behind us, but something from it had stayed, a sense of renewal. When I returned to the plant, I felt different. The same machines awaited me, the same noise, the same dust, but I wasn't dragging myself anymore. My mind felt lighter, my steps more certain.

I realized something profound during that trip: rest isn't a weakness, it is disguised strength. Without it, dedication decays into self-destruction. Just as we lubricate bearings to prevent seizure, life too demands lubrication, rest, laughter, time.

That one day off had done what a hundred lectures on stress management couldn't. It reminded me that even machines are given downtime, and I was no exception. From that day forward, I stopped glorifying exhaustion. I still worked hard, maybe harder. The city had given me more than memories; it had given me perspective. When the fan spun above me that night in my hostel room, I watched its blades whirl in perfect balance and smiled.

Chapter 2
The Plant Never Sleeps

The phone rang at 2:07 a.m. You'd think I'd be used to midnight calls by now. But they still jolted me awake and frightened me in a way no horror movie ever could. The ringtone somehow seemed shriller and sharper that night. My eyes snapped open, but my body lagged behind, caught between sleep and panic. My breath hitched in my chest, and the cold winter air slipped in through the half-open window. On the other end, the shift engineer's voice trembled with urgency. "Sir, the gear motor has failed. The entire section is down." I sat up, rubbing my eyes, trying to orient myself. The room was pitch dark except for the dim light from my phone. Outside, the plant siren howled faintly in the distance, an industrial wail that had become the soundtrack of my life.

I splashed water on my face, threw on my faded blue overalls, grabbed the hardhat hanging from a nail, and ran. The hostel corridor was silent except for the buzz of a tube light flickering overhead. My boots echoed down the narrow staircase. Within minutes, I was on the plant road, my breath fogging in the cold air. Throughout the drive from the hostel to the plant, my mind raced through a checklist faster than any engine could spin. *What failed exactly? Do we have a spare drive? A gearbox? A geared motor?* I remembered we had the gearbox, but not the geared motor. That gap felt like a hole in my chest.

By the time I reached the section, the air was already thick with the smell of burnt oil. Sparks flashed from handheld torches as technicians crowded around the dead equipment. The geared motor, massive, grey, and still radiating heat, sat lifeless like a fallen beast. The shift engineer briefed me quickly, "Sir, the motor tripped. We tried resetting it twice but no response. Checked drive signals. Dead. The temperature was 120 degrees before the trip." I knelt beside the gearbox, running my glove across the metal casing. It was still warm, too warm. "Shut down the section fully," I ordered. "Let's isolate and start inspection." The team jumped into action. Switches clacked, valves hissed, and in that orchestrated chaos, I felt the old rush of adrenaline. The electrician checked the drive panel. Another technician brought the Megger tester. The readings were clear: motor insulation had failed. I took a deep breath. "We'll need a replacement motor. Get in touch with the electrical store immediately." The call went out, but the response was the same we dreaded every time: "Sir, we don't have the same rating in stock." Silence followed. I looked at my watch. 3:36 a.m. The clock ticked like a reminder that every passing minute meant lost production.

"Alright," I said finally. "Let's think. What's available?"

"Sir, there's a lower-rated motor—about 80% of capacity."

"Let's try it."

That kicked off the next set of battle. The next few hours blurred into one long sequence of activity.

We called in the electrical team, whoever was available. Cables were unrolled across the floor like veins. Tools clattered. Someone fetched the crane, someone else fetched tea. The night turned into morning, then into noon. The lower-rated motor was mounted by 9 a.m. The moment of truth came when we started it. The drive hummed to life, gears began to rotate, and then, within seconds, the system tripped again. A sharp click followed by silence. "Drive under-rated," murmured the electrician. "Can't take the load." I pressed my palm against my forehead. Years later, I'd still remember that sound, the tripping relay echoing like a heart monitor flat-lining. "Try reducing torque," I said. "Adjust drive parameters, limit the current." We tried again. Another trip. Again. Trip. Each failed attempt cut deeper into our morale. By noon, exhaustion settled on everyone's faces. Eyes were red. Shoulders were slumped. We'd been running on nothing but tea and determination. I looked at the team, sweat-streaked, grease-smeared, half-dead, waiting for my next order. "Okay," I said quietly. "Everyone take a break. Let's think before we burn out another motor." I stepped outside for the first time in hours. The afternoon sun felt almost unreal, blinding after the dark interior. My hands shook as I poured water from my bottle. I hadn't eaten since dinner the night before.

Every breakdown had two parts, the visible mechanical failure and the invisible emotional one. The first could be fixed with spares; the second lingered silently inside every engineer who felt responsible. I called the store again, trying to arrange the higher-rated motor from another plant. The logistics were complicated due to different locations, transport availability, vendor lead time. Still, I pushed. I begged. I promised. I even argued with procurement. I finally sat down on an overturned drum near the machine. My head buzzed with fatigue, but my mind refused to rest. The plant lights shimmered through a thin haze of dust. Fatigue had blurred my judgment; another attempt might burn more than the motor. I called in one of my colleagues, Ravi, from the other shift. He was fresh, rested, and sharp-eyed. I gave him a quick hand-over, "The gearbox is intact. The drive trips instantly under torque. Electrical team has tested insulation, no faults on supply side. Only option now is higher-rated motor. Procurement is coordinating with the sister plant. Keep the area isolated till then. Don't attempt a restart." He nodded, reading the fatigue behind my tone. "Go rest, Shahbaz. We'll manage." For a second, I hesitated. Leaving a breakdown mid-way felt like abandoning a patient on the operating table. But the truth was, I had nothing left to give. My thoughts were stuttering; my eyes stung every time I blinked. "Call me if there's any update," I said, forcing a half-smile.

I peeled off my gloves, feeling the sting of air against raw palms, and walked out of the section. Each step toward the gate felt heavier than the one before. The sun outside was blinding, the world annoyingly normal, birds calling, workers chatting, life moving on while my mind was still trapped in the roar of the failed motor. Back at the hostel, I didn't even take off my shoes. I fell onto the bed and the world went black.

When I opened my eyes, the light outside was different. For a moment I couldn't tell if it was morning or evening. My phone buzzed beside me with a new message from Ravi, *"Motor arranged from sister plant. Higher rating. Installation in progress."* Relief arrived as a long, shaky exhale. My body was sore, my throat dry, but something inside finally unclenched. By the time I reached the plant later that night, the hum had returned. The new motor was mounted, cables neatly dressed, lubrication lines primed. The machine ran steady and smooth, as if mocking all our sleepless panic. Ravi grinned when he saw me. "Running beautifully," he said. "Temperature's perfect. No abnormal noise." I nodded, feeling a mix of pride and humility.

That night, lying in my hostel bed with the hum of the distant plant seeping through the walls, I replayed everything. The exhaustion, the fear of losing credibility, the frantic calculations, the helplessness. Each lost dispatch had felt like another nail in my professional coffin. I thought about my family and parents; how would I support them if I lost my income? Would I find another job quickly, or would it take months? The spiral of worry had pushed me into excessive stress, anxiety, and even high blood pressure. What lingered most wasn't the failure, it was the feeling of having reached my limit and then having to trust someone else to carry forward. In that moment I understood something fundamental: the plant never sleeps, but we must. Machines can run continuously; humans can't. When fatigue takes over, judgment evaporates, and even the best engineer turns into a hazard.

The very next day, our entire team was called in. The bosses' boss, Mr. Anupam, wanted answers: How did this happen? What was the root cause? Do we have enough spares? What's the lead time? Can we upgrade to a better design?

I explained what we had discovered, the inherent limitation of the vertical geared motor, the inadequate lubrication at the lower pinion, the thermal stress that built up unseen. Then I proposed an alternative: shift to a horizontal configuration or a separate gearbox-motor arrangement with forced lubrication. Instead of blame, I saw interest. Mr. Anupam nodded slowly. "Alright," he said, "let's not just repair it, let's redesign it. Shahbaz, you'll lead the project." For a heartbeat, I just stared at him. The same incident that had filled me with dread a day ago had now turned into an opportunity. My failure had earned me trust. As the meeting dispersed, I felt strangely light. The plant still roared in the background, indifferent to my little victories and breakdowns.

The following weeks became a blur of planning, procurement, and persistence. Drawings were made, revised, and rejected. Vendors were chased for dimensions, delivery dates, and quality certificates. Every small progress felt like a victory in a long siege. The workshop smelled of burnt electrodes and cutting oil as we prepared the new base frame and coupling assembly. We added an oil pump and heat exchanger to the gearbox, an innovation that would keep the bearings cool even in continuous duty. The new system was planned for installation during a scheduled plant shutdown in April. By then, every dimension had been checked twice, every lifting point rehearsed. When the day came, the shutdown felt like a coordinated symphony; scaffolders, electricians, riggers, mechanics, all moving with practiced urgency. As the old motor was lifted off its base, I ran my hand over its worn casing, a final gesture of respect. The new drive slid into position like it had always belonged there. Alignment readings were perfect. At 11:30 p.m., we powered it up. The motor came alive with a soft hum, smooth and steady. The gearbox rotated effortlessly, the oil sight glass glowing amber in the light. The team broke into smiles. I exhaled for what felt like the first time in weeks.

Lessons from that night:

- **Pressure is the profession's shadow:** That night taught me that pressure is not an interruption to the job; it *is* the job. Breakdowns arrive without warning, to test not your knowledge, but your temperament. In the beginning, I fought them with anxiety and resistance, believing that competence meant preventing every failure. Over time I learned the truth: you can't eliminate uncertainty in plant life, only prepare for it. Real professionalism lies in staying composed while the unexpected unfolds.

- **Stress distorts judgment; rest restores it:** When the motor tripped and calls started multiplying, my mind raced faster than any drive I had ever seen. Every scenario looked catastrophic, every failure felt personal. Fatigue blurred the line between reality and imagination. Only when I stepped away did clarity return. It was a simple lesson but one that many engineers ignore: the brain, like any bearing, overheats without lubrication. Rest, hydration, and distance are not luxuries; they are preventive maintenance for the mind. Managing machines begins with managing oneself.

- **Every crisis hides a blueprint for progress:** At its worst, that breakdown felt like the end of my credibility, as though one machine failure had erased years of effort. Yet, when the noise settled, it became the start of something new: a redesign project that improved reliability for years to come. That is how industry works. Every failure, if examined honestly, carries the seed of innovation. Crisis is the harshest but most effective teacher. You only have to listen long enough to translate its noise into learning.

- **No engineer wins alone:** That night I realized how fragile individual effort is. My knowledge, experience, and resolve would have meant nothing without the electrical team who refused to give up. They stayed through the night, adjusting cables, rewiring circuits, and bringing life back into the system. In manufacturing, heroism is never solitary; it is always collective. Success belongs to those who lift together, fail together, and show up again after twenty sleepless hours. Machines may run on power, but plants run on people.

- **Credibility is built in recovery, not in perfection:** Before that night, I thought credibility came from flawless performance. I was wrong. It is earned in the moments after things fall apart; in how you communicate, how you take responsibility, and how you guide others toward a solution. Nobody remembers how many smooth days the plant had; they remember who stood calm when chaos hit. Leadership is less about preventing breakdowns and more about being the steady hand that helps restart the system.

- **Balance is an operational requirement:** Anxiety and exhaustion were my real adversaries that night, invisible but far more dangerous than any mechanical fault. They dulled decision-making, shortened patience, and clouded vision. When I finally rested, I realized that balance isn't indulgence; it's insurance. A tired mind can trip faster than a relay. Since then, I have learned to treat calmness and health as part of reliability itself.

Weeks later, I would sometimes pause near that section, just to listen. The hum of the new motor was steady, unwavering, almost proud. And every time I heard it, I smiled to myself, because I knew what that sound meant. It was proof that the plant never sleeps.

Chapter 3
When Pressure Breaks

November 2015 was one of the happiest months of my life. I had just gotten married. Family, friends, and colleagues had gathered to celebrate a new beginning. But even on that day, as the lights glimmered and people congratulated us, part of my mind was still at the plant. I was smiling in photos while worrying about vibration levels in a gearbox and pending preventive jobs. The plant had become an extension of me, so much so that I forgot how to switch it off inside my head. Shaista, my wife, noticed this early on. The honeymoon period was short-lived. Within weeks she started saying softly, "You never have time for me." Sometimes she said it jokingly, sometimes with quiet hurt. My parents too had the same complaint. "You're living for the plant," my father told me once over a late-night call. "You visit home, but you're never *present*." I listened but didn't change. I told myself this was normal, that early career years demanded sacrifice. I had to prove myself, I thought. One day, all this effort would pay off.

Work became my only priority. I started believing that being busy was the same as being successful. Even on Sundays, I found reasons to visit the plant: "just to check." I convinced myself that my team needed me, that the machines would run smoother if I was around. Slowly, this habit turned into obsession. Shaista would wait for me at dinner. I would often return after midnight, too tired to talk. Some nights, I slept on the sofa with my laptop open, reports half-typed. On the few evenings we went out, my phone kept buzzing. Each call carried invisible chains pulling me back to the site. My wife's disappointment grew, but I kept telling her, "Just a few more months. Things will settle."

Sleep started slipping away. I'd lie in bed staring at the ceiling, replaying every detail of the day: the gearbox temperature, the lubrication issue, the spare shortage, the way my boss had frowned at a report. Even when I closed my eyes, my mind kept running like a motor that refused to stop. Gradually, fatigue took over. I began to lose focus. My memory dulled; even simple tasks required effort. Every small issue felt enormous. At work, I smiled outwardly, but inside, I was crumbling. My confidence started eroding, bit by bit. Inside me, a chemical war raged. Cortisol surged, adrenaline spiked, my body permanently stuck in fight-or-flight mode. Each phone call, each vibration alert, each emergency message triggered the same panic. My system was running like an overloaded circuit, and I was too afraid to pull the plug.

I remember reading later in Lori Gottlieb's *Maybe You Should Talk to Someone* about how we often build "a prison of our own making." At that time, I didn't need to read it, I was living it. My walls weren't built of concrete but of fear, guilt, and endless responsibility.

Every day the walls closed in a little more, and I didn't know how to escape.

Then came the night of another breakdown at the plant. The shift engineer called and without thinking, I threw on my jacket and rushed out. Shaista stirred in her sleep and mumbled, "Again?" Her voice was weary, not angry, just tired of this routine. I had no answer. The plant lights glared against the fog as I arrived. Steam hissed from the failed equipment. The same routine to trying to repair it followed. We didn't have all the spares. The required part was stored in another section, not immediately available. The safe option was to wait until morning for proper cooling and then proceed step-by-step. But this time, the pressure from above was intense; production loss, dispatch delay, phone calls from seniors. My mind screamed warnings. When I finally returned home, Shaista was standing at the door, worried. I said nothing. She looked at my tired face and whispered, "You're hurting yourself." I brushed it aside and collapsed into bed.

Two weeks later, the same issue returned. The same machine, the same section, another stoppage. This time, no excuse could protect me. The bosses were furious. My reporting manager called me in. His tone was calm but sharp. "Shahbaz," he said, "you're taking shortcuts. You're losing judgment under pressure. I'm losing trust." Those words cut deeper than any scolding ever could. Trust was everything to me. It was my oxygen. Hearing that it was slipping away left me gasping. I drove home that evening in silence. The road lights blurred. I parked outside my quarters, engine still running, and sat there for a long time staring at the dashboard. For the first time, I felt like quitting. But how could I walk away? The plant was my identity. Without it, who was I? That night, sleep didn't come. My mind looped endlessly between failure, fear, and fatigue. I was a prisoner of my own making; locked behind invisible bars, trapped between duty and despair.

The weeks after that confrontation felt heavy. I showed up every morning, did every inspection, prepared every report, but the energy was gone. I worked like a man carrying invisible weight on his shoulders. Sleep became a luxury I could no longer afford. Nights passed with my eyes open, staring into the dark, replaying that single sentence again and again—"I'm losing trust." Each time I heard those words echo in my head, my chest tightened. The thought of losing credibility terrified me more than losing comfort. Trust had been my currency, my proof that sleepless nights were worth it. And now that too seemed gone. I started avoiding people. Even casual conversation felt like exposure. In meetings, I nodded mechanically, rarely speaking. My appetite vanished for a while, then returned with vengeance, mindless eating at odd hours. My weight went up, my self-worth went down. Inside, I was crumbling.

But then came an unexpected test of a different kind. I was selected by a committee to present our monthly performance in a mass meeting. My stomach dropped. To most engineers, such a chance was an honour, even a career booster. But for me, at that moment, it felt like walking toward another breakdown.

I had stage fright. Even in school, I hated standing at the front of the class. Now, years later, I was being asked to present before hundreds, colleagues, managers, unit heads, even Mr. Arvind and Mr. Anupam. Instead of pride, dread filled me. I imagined myself freezing mid-sentence, stammering, forgetting numbers, making a fool of myself. The more I thought, the worse it grew. Still, there was no way out. Saying no would look like weakness. So I decided to prepare. Everywhere became my rehearsal room. In the washroom mirror, I practiced my opening line. In the car, I repeated data points like mantras. In the staircase, I imagined the audience in front of me. Sometimes I locked myself inside an empty container and spoke to the walls. At night, Shaista watched silently as I mumbled to myself, pacing the floor. She said softly, "You'll do fine. Just breathe." I nodded but didn't believe it. Sleep shrank to two hours a night. Every time I closed my eyes, I saw the stage lights glaring at me. The fear was physical even; sweaty palms, shaky legs, and dry mouth. My amygdala stayed on high alert, screaming *run!* long before I reached the auditorium.

Finally, the day came. The meeting hall was packed. Rows of employees filled the seats; the atmosphere buzzed with energy. The presenters were seated separately near the front. I could hear faint echoes of chatter, the click of projectors, the rustle of papers. When my name was announced— "Mr. Shahbaz Khan, Mechanical Department"— the world slowed down. I stood up, legs stiff, throat parched. My heart pounded so loud I could hear it in my ears. As I walked up, the lights hit my face like a spotlight of judgment. Holding the microphone, I looked at the crowd and blanked out completely. Every line I had practiced vanished. The slides blurred. My frontal lobe froze. The amygdala took over, whispering the same word it always does in fear: *escape.* For a second, I truly considered running off stage. Then, almost by instinct, I did the smallest thing possible. I spoke my name.

"My name is Shahbaz Khan... Mechanical Department."

I paused. Reached for the water glass on the table. Took a slow sip. The cold water hit my throat, oxygen reached my lungs, and something clicked back inside me. My breathing slowed. My mind began to function again. I looked at the slide, read the first line, and repeated it aloud. One line became another. One minute became five. Gradually, the room returned to focus. I started explaining performance charts, power consumption trends, downtime reduction, small reliability improvements. The audience nodded. A few even smiled. I felt my shoulders relax for the first time in weeks. Halfway through, applause broke out after a graph showing how our modification reduced stoppage hours. I glanced toward the front row. Mr. Arvind and Mr. Anupam were both smiling, nodding in approval. My fear melted, replaced by calm energy. I spoke the rest naturally, answering questions clearly, confident not from memory but from experience. When the session ended, the hall echoed with applause.

Later that day, during closing remarks, my name was announced again: "Best Presentation – Mechanical Department." For a moment, I sat frozen. The words barely sank in. When I walked back to my seat, colleagues patted my back, smiling. Some said, "You looked confident." I smiled back, but inside, I was in disbelief. Confident? I had been terrified. Yet somehow, through fear, I had found focus.

That night, for the first time in months, I slept peacefully. The next morning felt different. The sunlight didn't feel harsh; the air felt lighter. Even the routine plant noise seemed musical. It wasn't the award that had changed me, it was the realization behind it. Fear could be managed. Stress could be channelled. And trust could be rebuilt, not by words but by persistent action. I didn't become fearless overnight. I still felt nervous before every big review or shutdown meeting. But now I knew the trick to break fear into smaller parts. "Say your name. Take a breath. Start with one step. Momentum will take care of the rest." This simple truth became my anchor in the years that followed.

The next few weeks even moved differently. One evening, a junior engineer rushed into my cabin, panicked over a minor conveyor issue. I could see the same worry in his eyes that I once carried. Instead of snapping at him, I smiled and said, "Take a breath first. Machines respond better when minds are calm." It felt strange giving advice I'd only recently learned myself. The truth was, the fear hadn't disappeared, it had merely transformed. I still felt pressure, but it no longer consumed me. It became energy, something I could shape instead of something that shaped me.

At home, Shaista began to see the difference too. I returned earlier some evenings, and we sat together on the balcony sipping tea, watching the orange sky fade into night. Those quiet moments became my recharge time. One evening she said, "I know you're still working hard, but you've stopped punishing yourself for it. I am happy to see you like this." Her words stayed with me. For years, I had worked as though guilt was part of my job description; guilt for not doing enough, guilt for resting, guilt for wanting peace. But now I understood that peace was part of performance.

The lesson from that stage incident stayed in my mind like a formula: breathe, focus, proceed. Whenever a problem escalated, I used it. During shutdowns, inspections, or meetings, whenever I felt my heartbeat rise, I took a deep breath. The brain, I learned, resets with oxygen. That single breath could turn chaos into clarity. Slowly, my team began to notice the change. One of them said jokingly, "Sir, you've stopped shouting. You've become Zen!" We laughed, but there was truth in his words. The person who once lived on constant alert had finally found a rhythm. I even restarted reading. As I reread Lori Gottlieb's *Maybe You Should Talk to Someone*, a line caught my attention: "We can't always choose what happens to us, but we can choose how we respond." That line summarized my entire journey so far. I couldn't control breakdowns, bosses' attitudes, or production pressure but I could control my reaction.

Looking back, that entire phase of life felt like standing between two furnaces: one outside, one inside. The outer furnace was the plant's pressure; the inner one was my mind's turmoil. Both burned simultaneously until I learned how to regulate the flame. This phase of my journey revealed something profound to me, lessons that no training program or technical manual could ever teach.

- Fear never truly disappears; it only learns to coexist with courage. The trembling never fully goes away, but you learn to move despite it.
- Stress never vanishes; it transforms when given direction. Channelled properly, it sharpens focus instead of clouding it.
- Trust, once shaken, doesn't rebuild overnight, but persistence lays each brick back in place. Every small act of consistency restores what panic once broke.

Through those nights of breakdowns, failures, sleepless hours, and that single trembling moment on stage, I understood what resilience truly means. It isn't the absence of fear or failure. It's the quiet decision to rise again, even when your legs are shaking. It's choosing to breathe when panic tightens the chest, to think when emotion demands reaction, to keep faith when trust has cracked. Credibility, I realized, isn't built in moments of comfort or applause. It's forged in the furnace of discomfort, when pressure tests your limits and you still choose integrity over impulse. In fact, the plant never stopped testing me. But after that winter, I stopped fearing those tests. I learned that stress, like heat in a kiln, can either destroy or strengthen, depending on how you manage it. When pressure breaks, it doesn't have to end you. Sometimes it cracks open the version of you that's been waiting to emerge.

And that's what that year did for me; it redefined me.

Chapter 4
The Tea Hut and The Unseen Bonds

Whenever the noise of the plant grew unbearable I found myself walking down a familiar path beyond the main gate. The road curved slightly, past the guard post and a patch of wild grass, leading to a small bamboo hut. It was the same tea hut I remembered from my early days, back during my probation period. Back then, we'd sit on the plank balanced on old paint tins, exhausted after 16-hour shifts. The hut, with its smoky roof and glass jars full of biscuits and farali chevdo, had felt like a luxury and routine at the same time.

Years later, the hut is exactly where it had been. Bamboo sticks tied together with rusted wire, its roof patched with blackened tarpaulin, one corner slightly torn where sunlight streamed in. The same old coal blower wheezed beside the counter, puffing out bursts of air into the fire that licked beneath the kettle. The air smelled of burnt coal, boiling milk, and sweet tea leaves. The old owner, Lakhubhai, still ran the place. His white vest was darkened by smoke, and his voice was rough. “Same tea, Babu?” he would ask, smiling. “Yes, same tea” I would say, smiling. He nodded knowingly, as if time hadn’t passed at all. He took a ladle, stirred the bubbling kettle, and poured the amber-coloured liquid through a steel sieve into a glass.

I took my usual place on the bench and stared at the world around me. Trucks rumbled toward the loading bay. Labourers walked past, their faces streaked with dust, eyes tired but determined. A few laughed among themselves, sipping tea before another long shift. I wrapped both hands around my glass, inhaling the steam. Each sip burned my tongue slightly but also melted the tension, the fatigue, the invisible pressure. Beside my glass sat three small packets of *farali chevdo* and a handful of Kutch *badam*, my ritual order. I’d open one packet slowly, chew quietly, and let my thoughts rearrange themselves.

That was the beauty of the tea hut, it wasn’t about tea; it was about space. It gave me permission to pause, to breathe between crises, to step back from the storm and see the bigger picture. When the fog in my mind cleared, I took out my pocket diary which I carried everywhere (inspired by our very own diary-king, Mr. Manohar). In that small notebook, I wrote everything: shutdown schedules, spare requirements, ideas for efficiency, and sometimes, even my frustrations. The diary became both a technical log and an emotional vent, a habit that grounded me more than meditation ever could. After fifteen minutes of tea, silence, and scribbling, I would walk back toward the plant, calmer and ready to face the chaos again.

The habit became a pattern, and soon, I began to notice something remarkable. Whenever I took these small pauses, my productivity actually increased. My thoughts sharpened, my decisions grew clearer, and my temper softened. So I brought the tea-hut principle inside the plant. Instead of forcing my team to power through every crisis without rest, I began encouraging short breaks, group discussions, and idea-sharing sessions. At first, they thought I'd gone soft. But when shutdown jobs began finishing faster and more safely, they understood. During one planning meeting, when I told my shop-floor team, "Everyone here has ideas and every idea matters," there was an awkward silence at first. In the hierarchy of plant life, suggestions usually flowed downward, not upward. But I waited. Finally, Neel, our machinist, spoke up. "Sir, we should order spare gaskets before every shutdown. Always the same issue." Then Ghanshyam, a wiry, quick-thinking fitter, added, "We can modify the hardware to reduce vibration on the drive coupling." Even the quiet ones joined in. Rajeev, our thinnest and most daring technician, suggested keeping a second team ready for confined-space work. I wrote every point in my diary. I even asked everyone to start keeping small notebooks of their own. Some smiled, others shrugged, but soon I noticed them writing during shifts, jotting reminders, noting down problems. Those small diaries changed our culture. We began to work like an orchestra, every section tuned, every instrument in sync. During shutdowns, manpower was pre-assigned, spares arranged in advance, tools checked, and vendor calls made ahead of time. Torque wrenches, extension rods, universal joints, and electric wrenches, everything was lined up like soldiers before battle. When the next major job came, we executed it like clockwork. Over 3,000 bolts and nuts were tightened and loosened within two days. There was laughter, focus, and even pride on faces that had once known only fatigue.

It was during one of those long shifts that a small incident changed the way I saw my team forever. We were working inside the cooler section, replacing liner plates. Rajeev volunteered to crawl into a narrow space where the bolts were nearly impossible to reach. I watched him squeeze himself between two beams, his helmet scraping the steel. He looked almost weightless, arms stretched, sweat dripping. When he emerged, I decided to try it myself, wanting to understand what it felt like. But halfway in, I got stuck. My belly pressed against the beam, and I couldn't move. "Sir!" Rajeev laughed, clutching his side. "You'll need a hydra to pull yourself out!" The team burst out laughing, and even I couldn't help it. In that small, embarrassing moment, I realized how little we, as supervisors, understood the physical grind our men endured every single day. We stood outside, giving instructions and chasing deadlines, but they lay inside machines, breathing dust, risking burns, crawling through spaces no engineer's ego could fit into. That realization stayed with me.

As I dusted off my helmet, I looked up. Mr. Shyam, who had been cleaning clinker on the upper platform, smiled and extended a hand to pull me up. His palms were rough, covered in calluses, but his touch carried warmth. He grinned and said softly, “Sir, all we need sometimes is a little tea, snacks, and water when we’re working inside. That’s enough to keep us going.” I nodded immediately. “Done, Shyam.” And that was how a bond began.

From that day on, Shyam became more than just a helper on the floor. My experience with Shyam can best be expressed through the words of Albert Schweitzer: “Sometimes our light goes out, but is blown again into instant flame by an encounter with another human being.” He was always around, sometimes sweeping near the machine, sometimes checking water drums, and sometimes quietly waiting outside the control room with a glass of tea. I began noticing small things. My table was always clean, files stacked neatly, even my chair wiped every morning. If I reached the plant late, there would already be a cup of tea placed at the corner of my desk, still steaming. At first, I thought it was coincidence or initiative from housekeeping. But then I realized it was Shyam. One afternoon, as I was finalizing shutdown reports, he came by holding a duster. “Sir, permission to clean?” he asked. I laughed. “You don’t need permission for that, Shyam.” He smiled shyly, cleaned the table with slow, precise strokes, and before leaving said, “Sir, don’t skip lunch today. I saw you didn’t go to the canteen.” That stopped me. In a plant where most people barely had time to look up from their monitors, someone had actually noticed that I hadn't eaten.

With time, his acts of care multiplied in quiet, invisible ways. One evening, after an exhausting 14-hour shutdown, I returned home to find my car washed and parked perfectly. The windshield was spotless; even the wipers had been lifted so they wouldn't stick overnight. The next day, it happened again. And again. Finally, I confronted him gently.

"Shyam, you don't have to do that. You already have enough on your plate." He simply said, "Sir, when I clean your car, it feels like I'm cleaning a bit of my own stress." I didn't know how to respond.

He began showing up near my quarters occasionally. One weekend, my wife called out from the kitchen, laughing. "There's a man helping me cook! He's passing spices as if he's part of the family." When I walked in, I found Shyam standing there, sleeves rolled up, handing her cumin and coriander like a careful apprentice. "Shyam!" I said, half shocked, half amused.

He smiled awkwardly. "Just helping, Sir. Madam is making khichdi. I told her little more ghee makes it better." We all laughed. But behind that laughter, I felt a kind of affection that blurred the line between professional and personal life. Shyam wasn't crossing boundaries. He was building bridges. He had seen me at my worst, angry, anxious, sleep-deprived, and still looked at me with the same quiet respect.

Over the next few months, his gestures became almost ritualistic. Every morning, before the shift meeting, he'd appear near my desk with tea. Every Friday, he'd sweep the corners of the office, mumbling small prayers. Every inspection day, he'd polish my helmet till it shone like new. Once, during the monsoon, he even stood outside my car with an umbrella when I was leaving the plant. Rain soaked him, but he refused to move until I was safely inside. Leadership books talk about engagement, motivation, and emotional intelligence. But standing there, with rain falling between us, I realized something they never teach: "care is the purest form of leadership."

A few days later, we were having tea together at the same hut. It had become a shared ritual now, the manager and the workman, sitting side by side, sipping from glasses that looked identical. The steam from our cups blurred the line between rank and hierarchy. "Sir," he said suddenly, eyes fixed on the coal fire, "when you get promoted again, you'll be transferred, right?" I nodded. "Maybe. That's how it works." He looked down, stirred his tea, and said in a low voice, "Then who will take care of you there?" The question caught me off guard.

"I'll take care of myself, Shyam." He smiled faintly. "No, Sir. People like you forget to do that." He wasn't wrong. For years, I had been so focused on meeting targets, handling crises, and proving myself that I had forgotten how to rest, how to receive care without guilt. In his own simple way, Shyam reminded me that leadership wasn't only about giving. It was also about allowing others to give back.

Our friendship became an anchor during my toughest days. Whenever I faced stress from production pressure or criticism from seniors, he was there. He reminded me that even when machines dominate your world, humanity still finds a way to seep through. And in that quiet companionship, I began to heal from years of imbalance I had once thought permanent.

The months that followed were some of the most stable of my career. The plant was running smoothly, shutdowns were efficient, and even the senior management had begun to notice the improvement in teamwork. For the first time in years, I felt a balance inside myself. Much of that balance, I realized, came from people like Shyam. He never demanded recognition, but his presence kept everything grounded. If I was tense, he sensed it before I spoke. If morale was low, he'd somehow spark laughter among the men by cracking small jokes in Gujarati or teasing the welders about who drank the most tea. His loyalty was quiet, but his influence was loud.

Over time, my day began to revolve unconsciously around him. I'd arrive at the plant expecting the chair to be clean, the table to be dust-free, and my tea cup waiting. Even my family grew fond of him. My wife would often ask, "Has Shyam eaten today?" or "Tell him the khichdi turned out good because of his advice!" Sometimes, when I came home late, I'd find the parking area swept, the plants watered, or a small steel bowl of tea leaves left near the gate, a silent reminder that someone still cared for details others overlooked. I had told him not to trouble himself so many times, but he'd simply smile and say, "Sir, this is my happiness. Don't take it away." There was no arguing with that kind of sincerity.

When the official announcement of my promotion and transfer came, it felt like a moment I had worked years for. Yet, strangely, there wasn't the kind of joy in me that I had expected. I had always dreamed of moving to a larger plant, handling bigger responsibilities. But now that it was real, I couldn't help thinking of what I'd be leaving behind, the routines, the laughter, the people who had stood beside me through every breakdown and every night shift. And among them all, one face kept appearing in my mind — Shyam's. I didn't know how to tell him. When he found out through others, he appeared at the door holding a glass of tea. His eyes were red, though he was smiling. "Congratulations, Sir," he said softly. "You deserve this." "Thank you, Shyam," I replied, unsure what else to say. He looked down for a moment, then said, "When you go, this place will miss you." "I'll miss it too," I said. He nodded again and added, "And I'll miss you more than this place." His words hit deeper than I expected.

The day of my farewell arrived like any other morning, dusty air, rumbling machines, and distant truck horns. But beneath the normalcy, emotion ran thick. By noon, the workshop was decorated with streamers and banners. Colleagues gathered, laughter echoing awkwardly as everyone tried to keep things cheerful. Speeches were made, the usual mix of praise, nostalgia, and corporate humour. Someone mentioned how I had turned a struggling unit into an efficient team. Another joked about my obsession with torque wrenches and diaries. But through it all, I kept glancing toward the back of the crowd, searching for one face. And there he was standing quietly near the doorway, wearing his best uniform, a faint stain of grease still on his sleeve. He wasn't clapping. He wasn't smiling. He was just... watching. When it was my turn to speak, I said all the expected words, gratitude to the management, appreciation for the team, hope for the future. But as I looked at the people before me, my eyes stopped on Shyam. And suddenly, the rehearsed words disappeared. My voice wavered. "Sometimes in life," I said, "we

think machines are what keep the plant running. But the truth is, it's people, the ones who care, who show up every day, who go beyond their duty without ever asking for anything." I didn't take his name. I didn't need to. Everyone turned to look at him anyway. For a long second, our eyes met. He smiled faintly, and then looked down, rubbing his hands together. The same hands that had cleaned my desk, washed my car, passed my wife the cumin seeds, and carried more unseen kindness than anyone could measure.

After the ceremony, I walked toward the gate. My car was packed; the papers signed. The driver waited, engine running. Then I saw Shyam standing near the exit, holding a small bag wrapped in old newspaper. He approached silently, extended it toward me, and said, "For you, Sir." I unwrapped it. Inside was a glass cup, the kind used at the tea hut, slightly chipped at the rim, stained from years of use. "This was yours," he said. "You always used the same one there. I kept it safe." For a moment, I couldn't speak. My throat tightened. I placed a hand on his shoulder. "Shyam," I managed, "thank you… for everything." He shook his head. "No, Sir. Thank you, for seeing me." Then, unable to hold back, he bent down and touched my feet. Tears streamed down his face. I stopped him immediately, pulling him into an embrace. His body trembled like that of a child trying not to cry. When we finally stepped apart, I saw that the entire housekeeping team was watching, silently. No one said a word. But I knew, they understood. As my car rolled away, I looked back through the rear-view mirror. Shyam stood where I'd left him, the wind blowing dust around his figure. Slowly, he raised his hand in farewell. That image, a man standing in gray dust, waving silently, burned itself into my memory.

When I think back on those years now, the tea hut feels like more than just a place. It was a mirror of how far I had come, and how much I still had to learn. In my early days, I had looked at that hut as a place to escape chaos of the plant and the chaos in my mind. Years later, it became the place where I learned to breathe, to listen, to think. It gave me space. And through Shyam, it gave me soul. Lori Gottlieb, in Maybe You Should Talk to Someone, wrote that "we can't have change without loss, which is why so often people say they want change but nonetheless stay exactly the same." My bond with Shyam showed me this truth. I resisted change for so long, chained to stress and overthinking, yet real strength came from connections I never expected.

Shyam taught me that leadership isn't about authority, it's about empathy. That respect isn't demanded, it's earned through understanding. That loyalty isn't built through orders, it's built through care. Small rituals like a glass of tea can restore clarity under pressure. Small gestures of kindness can change the rhythm of an entire team. And sometimes, the greatest motivation doesn't come from awards or promotions, but from knowing that someone quietly prays for your well-being. Even today, whenever I walk past a roadside tea hut, the smell of boiling milk and coal smoke takes me back to those dusty mornings. I can almost hear the hiss of the blower, the clink of glasses, and the quiet voice saying, "Sir, don't forget to eat."

And as Maya Angelou once said: "People will forget what you said, people will forget what you did, but people will never forget how you made them feel." That was Shyam's gift to me. He made me feel cared for, even when I thought I was alone. A reminder that behind every machine, every process, every achievement, there are unseen bonds that keep everything alive. And no matter how far I travel, I carry that bond with me, as steady as the aroma of tea that never truly fades.

Chapter 5
Life in The Colony

If the plant was a monster that never slept, our residential colony was a fairyland. It was like a miniature republic built by engineers who had once read too much about town planning and decided to test their theories on real humans. The colony stretched over acres, its roads built so wide it seemed even the plant's trucks could rest there without crowding the space. At night, the tall sodium lights cast a

soothing amber glow. Each block was a kingdom of hierarchy. The 1BHK quarters were for fresh recruits, the "civilian population." The 2BHKs, like ours, belonged to the "middle class of survival." The 3BHKs were reserved for the ruling elite, i.e. the section heads and managers. But the true diversity of the colony lay not in its architecture, but in its inhabitants. The colony was a carnival of humanity. Here, a Bengali electrician lived next to a Punjabi fitter, who lived next to a Tamil instrument engineer, who lived opposite a Gujarati canteen contractor.

And then there was the wildlife. The peacocks were our unofficial morning alarms, honking from the boundary wall. Stray dogs ran supply chain operations for leftover rotis. Occasionally, an owl sat on the lamp post during night shifts. But the real celebrities were the monitor lizards. Long, muscular, prehistoric creatures that walked like retired wrestlers. One day, when a particularly confident specimen entered my quarter through an open door, the event became the "Lizard Emergency of Block C." It started with a rustling near the shoe rack. Shaista saw the tail first, and before I could finish the word "lizard," she had teleported onto the dining table like an Olympic high-jumper. I, not to be outdone in courage, leapt onto the bed. The lizard, meanwhile, had no idea it was the villain. It ran under the bed in panic. We tried everything, banging, shooing, pleading, but the creature stayed put. Finally, applying classical engineering logic, we sealed every door and left the main one open. Then we sat in silence, eyes fixed like two hostages negotiating peace. Minutes later, it cautiously emerged, gave us a long contemptuous look, and marched out into freedom. For a moment, we both exhaled like survivors of a mild natural disaster. Shaista declared that from now on, all doors would remain shut even if oxygen ran out. The colony was full of such adventures. Once, I spotted a porcupine scuttling near the wall at midnight, its spines shining like fibre-optic cables. Another time, while driving to the plant, I saw a tortoise crossing the road. I stopped, picked it up gently, and placed it in the pond nearby. For the rest of the day, I felt morally elevated, like a monk in overalls.

At one end stood the Shopping Complex. It had a grocery shop, barber, vegetable vendor, tailor, a photocopy corner that also sold toffees, and an ice-cream shop run by an old man. His mango dolly bars were a hit. In the middle of the complex was a big lawn with a dolphin-fish statue that looked neither like a dolphin nor a fish, but everyone agreed it was the colony's Eiffel Tower. "Meet me at the dolphin" became a catchphrase. Evenings were our social renaissance. Children cycled in circles; elders strolled with folded hands behind their backs, discussing politics, bonuses, and cricket. The women's laughter echoed from balconies, mixing with the whirr of ceiling fans and the scent of frying pakoras. Life, for once, seemed generous.

When Shaista and I first moved in, we were outsiders, two newcomers surrounded by established friendships. But the colony had its own gravitational pull. Within weeks, we were attending evening walks, Saturday tea gatherings, and Sunday pot-lucks where everyone judged everyone's pulao but complimented it anyway. Slowly, that patch of land became our small universe filled with half chaos and half comfort.

If the colony had one universal truth, it was this — nothing was ever permanent. People came, got promoted, got transferred, and left the colony for another one in another town. The only thing that stayed behind was their reputation. When word spread that I was next in line for transfer, the entire colony turned into a social calendar. Suddenly, we were the most wanted couple in the postal code. Dinner invitations poured in faster than HR circulars before Diwali. It started with Mr. Uday's dinner, the gentleman with a heart so big he could have been declared a renewable resource of kindness. He called us one evening with his signature line: "Sir, today you are not allowed to say no. Only allowed to say wow." At his house, the aroma of paneer and jeera rice floated through the air. Shaista, ever the perfectionist, had prepared an assortment of her homemade pickles as a parting gift. After dinner, as the plates were being cleared, she and Mrs. Uday shared a tender, teary-eyed moment. Her closest companions were part of the colony's legendary "Chandaal Chaukadi," a self-proclaimed, unapologetic gang of four women who fought monotony like freedom fighters. Every evening they assembled for their sacred "walk," a ritual that scientifically consisted of three minutes of actual walking and fifty-seven minutes of world-class gossip. They were, in short, the emotional Wi-Fi of the colony, everyone connected, everyone online. She was emotional the whole way back to our house.

The next invitation came from Mr. Salim, the undisputed King of Biryani and my friendly rival in what we called the "Coal Mill Eating Championship." His biryani wasn't food. It was an emotion layered in saffron and ghee. He greeted me with a grin: "Today, no diet, no guilt, only glory." And glory it was. We ate like men possessed, two rice mountains disappearing under the combined efficiency of two engineers trained in optimization. By the end, my stomach had expanded enough to apply for a separate PIN code. I lay down on the mat, unable to move, declaring myself "mechanically unavailable for further operations." Shaista rolled her eyes while Mrs. Salim handed her hajmola like first aid. Laughter filled the room. Even after all the dinners and farewells, that night stood out. Later, our friend Mr. Ashok brewed tea and served it in small disposable glasses. The simple drink revived us instantly, laughter flowing late into the night.

A few evenings later, I received the most unexpected invitation of all, from my boss, Mr. Arvind. The man was a legend, part myth, part policy. Naturally, I was nervous. Bosses rarely invite subordinates for dinner. But that night, something was different. Mr. Arvind wasn't the intimidating figure from the plant. He told stories from his early days, how he once worked through a 48-hour breakdown on nothing but tea and samosas, how his first presentation bombed hard. I remember how he chuckled when he said he presented a wrong report in front of the MD and spent an entire week convinced his career was over. "But guess what," he said, smiling, "nobody remembers that mistake except me." I listened, surprised, amused, and oddly comforted. For years, I had seen him as a machine in human form. But that evening, I met the man inside the title. When dinner was served, I forgot all protocol and asked for seconds. He laughed a genuine, warm laugh I had never heard at work. "You're the only one who eats like me," he said. "Maybe that's why you survived this plant so long." He laughed hard, I did too. I left his home that night with something rarer than a promotion: mutual respect born of understanding.

Back home, the house was turning into a cardboard forest. Boxes, tape, bubble wrap, all battling for space. Each corner carried an echo of memory. Every evening felt like a countdown. One less walk, one less dinner, one less lazy tea in the balcony. The colony, once just an address, had turned into a feeling. Leaving it felt like shutting down a living machine that had kept us human among the hum of motors. But as I sealed the final box, I reminded myself, engineers are nomads by profession. After the last farewell dinner, I found myself sitting alone on the balcony one night. The colony lay silent, bathed in the same amber glow of the streetlights. Somewhere, a peacock gave its usual dramatic cry. Across the road, Mr. Uday's porch light flickered. Kids were still playing cricket somewhere, shouting appeals. The air smelled faintly of night jasmine. How peaceful it felt to simply exist!

In Maximum Brainpower, Shlomo Breznitz and Collins Hemingway show that the human brain performs best not under continuous strain but through deliberate rest, that mental breaks are not interruptions in performance, but prerequisites for it. At the plant in my earlier days, I used to dismiss such ideas as academic theory. The kiln didn't rest, the conveyors didn't nap, and neither could we. Rest, in my view then, was a luxury for poets, not engineers. But the colony changed that philosophy entirely. I began to notice that some of my sharpest insights came not during high-pressure meetings or technical breakdowns, but during completely unrelated moments; over a cup of tea, while walking around the dolphin circle, or laughing at Ashok's wild theories about ghosts haunting the clinker silo. In those moments, something always clicked. I realized that all the heavy lifting of thought doesn't happen when we're forcing it. It happens when the mind gets permission to breathe. Breznitz was right: rest wasn't the enemy of efficiency; it was its foundation.

Around that same time, I started reading Dr. Gabor Maté's The Myth of Normal, a book that spoke straight to my industrially-conditioned soul. Maté warns that chronic stress and social disconnection carve invisible wounds into us. He explains how the modern world confuses achievement with health, and loneliness with independence. I could see those wounds everywhere around me. In the plant, many of my colleagues looked like walking stress tests. They arrived early, skipped meals, stayed late, and spoke of targets as if they were divine commandments. Their humour had evaporated, replaced by caffeine and compliance. Even I wasn't far behind. The colony became my antidote. It reminded me that human connection is preventive maintenance for the soul. Shaista's Chandaal Chaukadi was proof of that. Watching those four women laugh uncontrollably over trivial gossip was like witnessing a live therapy session conducted by stand-up comedians. Their laughter, unfiltered and spontaneous, could cure anything from bad moods to migraine. Shaista often returned from those walks lighter, glowing even, as if she had downloaded joy straight into her system. Her mood would uplift mine without her trying. I began to suspect that the human nervous system was contagious, one person's calm could reboot another's chaos. When she cried about leaving her friends, I understood it wasn't just sentiment. It was biology. She was mourning the loss of her support system, her nightly dose of community medicine. It struck me that this place had been less a residence and more a quiet teacher. It taught in gestures of the neighbour who left food by the door, the boss who suddenly seemed mortal, and the peace of the late evenings. In those unspoken lessons lay the essence of balance. As I prepared to leave, I knew that what I carried forward were not memories of events, but understandings shaped by them; truths that would stay with me throughout my personal and professional life.

1. Rest restores power. There is a kind of strength that comes only through stillness. I learned this in the last evenings of the colony, when work no longer chased me, and the hours seemed to expand again. The mind, once clenched around schedules and shutdowns, began to breathe. In those days, rest no longer felt like indulgence. I learnt that the brain, when allowed to idle, rearranges chaos into clarity. I noticed how ideas that once refused to appear during long meetings would visit me quietly while I sat with a cup of tea among friends and neighbours at the shopping complex. The pause itself became productive. The colony had its own rhythm. The sun rose over wide roads washed clean by the

night breeze; children cycled past lawns that glowed faintly under morning mist. Each evening the same roads turned into a walking track for men and women returning from the plant. There was slowness there, a deliberate pace that calmed the nervous system and reset the senses. At work, fatigue used to feel like a badge of honour. In the colony, it began to feel like waste. I learned that a rested mind is sharper than a strained one. A short nap could restore more focus than a night of forced effort. Even a dinner with friends, filled with laughter, worked like a reset switch. There was power in stepping away, and I began to see rest not as escape, but as strategy. Hence, I began to value silence. Sometimes I would sit outside after everyone slept, listening to the hum of insects and the distant bark of dogs. That stillness carried an intelligence of its own. It taught me that performance improves not through endless effort, but through rhythm: exertion followed by renewal, tension followed by release.

2. Community heals. The colony's real architecture was not its houses, but its connections. Every block, every lane carried stories of empathy and belonging. It was a world where fatigue softened in conversation and isolation dissolved over cups of evening tea. I saw how community functions as invisible medicine. Stress that felt unbearable alone became lighter when spoken aloud. This community created a fabric of

belonging that the workplace alone could never provide. When farewells began, I saw how strong those threads were. Every invitation, every meal carried the tenderness of something ending. Community, I realized, does not heal by solving problems. It heals by reminding you that you are not alone in them. The colony showed me how companionship steadies the mind. Even casual gestures like a neighbour waving and smiling from their front porch became acts of quiet repair. We are shaped by such gestures. They build a sense of safety that no job title can offer. When people around you care, stress loses its grip. The colony's laughter, gossip, and shared fatigue became a form of collective therapy.

3. Leaders are human too. Earlier I saw leadership as a distant peak, something cold, untouchable, and defined by authority. The dinner with my boss stayed with me. I began to see how leadership grows from transparency. When a senior opens up about uncertainty it builds mutual respect and understanding. It makes connection possible. The plant culture had taught me to hide exhaustion and doubt; the colony showed me that acknowledging them makes a leader more real. After that night, I noticed subtle changes in myself. I stopped pretending to be tireless. I began to listen more. When juniors hesitated to speak, I empathized. Leadership, I realized, is less about control and

> more about presence, the ability to make others feel safe enough to contribute. The colony even offered daily lessons in that kind of humility. You could not remain detached when your neighbours were the same people you worked with. Hierarchies blurred when everyone's children played together, when the same people who signed your reports borrowed your pressure cooker. Living among colleagues transformed my professional mechanical relationships into human ones.

As I helped load the last of the boxes into the back of the moving truck, I turned to look around the empty room of our quarter. I walked from room to room, switching off lights slowly. The echo of my own footsteps felt foreign. The colony had done something no city, no hostel, no plant could do, it had filled me with a sense of wholeness, a completeness that comes only from belonging. I wished I could pack that feeling into the suitcase along with my clothes, to open it again wherever the next posting took me. Our neighbours had gathered. Mr. Salim cracked a half-smile and said, "The next biryani will have to wait for your visit back." His wife pressed a box of sweets into Shaista's hands. Mrs. Chanda wiped her eyes discreetly, pretending to adjust her dupatta. When the driver started the engine, a hush fell. The truck moved forward with a slow groan, and the faces blurred behind a film of tears. We got into the car. Shaista turned once more to wave. A few neighbours raised their hands in response, small silhouettes framed against the yellow glow of the poles. When we finally rolled out of the colony gate, the night seemed unusually tender. The streetlights trailed behind like old companions seeing us off, their glow receding slowly until only darkness remained. And in that darkness I felt a quiet gratitude.

Chapter 6
The Pilot Pump Mystery

After Gujarat, the company decided I had been sufficiently roasted and ready for a new flame. My next destination was Rajasthan. Another unit of factory, another geography, another round of anxiety neatly wrapped in opportunity. The first thing that struck me about this new plant was its reputation. It wasn't just any unit, it was *the* "branding plant." People spoke of it in reverent tones, as if it were an Ivy League for cement engineers. The rumour was that once you survived here, your name carried a different weight in internal corridors. On my joining day, I was greeted with the kind of welcome that only manufacturing units can offer: a dusty handshake and a problem waiting for ownership. I was assigned to the LS Crusher section. It was where limestone entered the plant and good intentions went to die. Within weeks, I began to understand the all the tantrums and mood swings of the crusher. My early troubleshooting attempts won me small nods from seniors, the rare currency of manufacturing respect. When the section finally stabilized under my watch, I was promoted, or rather, *transferred upwards*, to the Raw Mill.

That transfer, I would later realize, was an initiation. The Raw Mill at this unit was legendary for all the wrong reasons. Four plants shared one site, and each line had its own set of chronic ailments. The place throbbed with stress, from the hum of conveyors to the constant calls from the control room. If Gujarat had taught me endurance, Rajasthan was going to teach me perspective. The Raw Mill itself was an architectural marvel. Everything was always in motion: belts, chains, hoppers, and people running between them with spanners in hand and worry in eyes. The air carried the faint perfume of hot oil and pressure. I quickly understood why this unit was called a "branding plant." It branded you all right. With sleepless nights, frayed nerves, and permanent dark circles. But it also carved your technical instincts sharper than any textbook could. Every engineer who walked out of here carried the mark of survival that was a blend of competence and mild trauma.

The first few days were pure observation. I roamed through sections with a diary, noting down repetitive problems: belt drifts, overloading trips, oil leakages, worn pulleys, eccentric shafts, and operators who prayed before pressing start. The Raw Mill, I realized, didn't need maintenance but therapy. It was during one of these walks that I saw it: a belt conveyor near the hopper building running in a condition that defied engineering dignity. The belt was so thin, light shone through it. It flapped like paper in the wind, drifted like a confused teenager, and triggered tripping alarms as if practicing Morse code. Every five minutes, the control room would call: "Sir, the belt tripped." The maintenance log showed months of makeshift repairs. I stood there for a moment, watching the belt wobble like an exhausted marathoner, and made a call that would set the tone for my time in Rajasthan. "Replace it today." The shift in-charge blinked. "Today, sir? It will take at least sixteen hours." "Then start now," I said, trying to sound braver than I felt. We arranged spares, lined up the crew, borrowed a hydra, and began the operation. By late night, the new belt was running smooth, straight and silent. The next morning, when I walked past the hopper, the belt hummed like a well-fed cat. For once, the control room was quiet. That rare silence felt divine. For about twenty-four hours, I allowed myself to believe I was in control. Then the universe remembered it was Rajasthan.

Two days later, the phone rang again. "Sir, counterweight has fallen." Translation: the conveyor's heart had detached and fallen, slicing the belt clean through. My heart followed the same trajectory. There's a special kind of panic that comes when you know the breakdown has your name on it. Palms sweat, pulse races, logic evaporates. You imagine bosses asking questions you don't have answers to, senior managers calling from nowhere, and HR silently updating termination probability charts. I reached the site breathless. The counterweight had indeed fallen, lying half-buried like a crime scene relic. The belt, a fresh casualty. The team stood around waiting for orders, faces pale under helmet lights. "Okay," I said, exhaling. "Let's start." That became the motto of my Rajasthan chapter: *heart racing, mind blank, still start.* Hours turned into nights. One breakdown led to another. The Raw Mill had a peculiar appetite, it chewed confidence and spat humility. But strangely, I was beginning to enjoy it. Somewhere in the stress was a strange clarity: every time I solved something, I grew.

Weeks later, another call came. This time the chain conveyor tail shaft had failed. Same script, same pulse, same panic. But now I knew the choreography. I rushed, assessed, delegated, executed. We worked till morning, hands black with oil, faces bright with relief when the system ran again. It was exhausting, yes. But addictive too. The Raw Mill was turning me into what I had always wanted to be; a man who could handle chaos without losing his calm. At least, that's what I told myself.

At home, my wife began to notice the tremor in my voice when the phone rang. "You look like you've seen a ghost," she teased once. "In a way," I said. "It's called a breakdown call." It became our running joke. Every time she suggested an outing, I felt my body tense. It was as if the machines had a sixth sense and they knew when we left the colony. "Let's go shopping," she said one Sunday, tired of my excuses. Two hours later, just as we were looking at curtains, the phone buzzed: "Sir, elevator bush gone." I stared at her helplessly. She stared back, then burst out laughing. "You and your machines have some karmic connection," she said. Her laughter was contagious, but deep down, I wanted to cry. The plant had invaded my life. My holidays had become predictive maintenance schedules.

I didn't know it yet, but the real test was waiting, the one that would define not just my technical ability, but my endurance as a human being. The test had a name and a price tag of one crore rupees. The morning the Raw Mill died felt like the planet itself had stopped rotating. The SKS hydraulic drive, our pride, our nightmare, had suddenly gone silent. I reached the site in minutes. The control room looked like a war bunker. Screens blinked red, alarms flashed, and everyone spoke in half-sentences. The shift engineer ran toward me, words tumbling over each other. "Sir, system pressure zero. No flow. The main pump isn't responding." For a few seconds, I just stared at the display, hoping it would miraculously fix itself. "All right," I said finally, "we'll start from scratch. Check oil level, filters, coupling, suction line." We checked everything. Nothing worked. The pump was lifeless. By evening, the tension had settled in. Mr. Ravi, the senior-most boss, arrived on site. He was a man of few words and many expectations. When he looked at the silent mill, it felt like judgment day. "What's the status?" he asked, calm but heavy. I began explaining the technical sequence, but his silence said it all. Two days had already passed. Two days of the entire plant waiting, dispatches delayed, losses multiplying. When pressure doesn't come from hydraulics, it comes from management. Finally, a decision was made: replace the main hydraulic pump.

The replacement itself was an operation worthy of a movie. The pump weighed as much as a small car, buried in a maze of pipes, flanges, and cables. Removing it meant disassembling half the drive. We began at dawn, a full army of technicians, riggers, welders, and electricians. The hydra stood like a loyal beast, its hook swaying under the weight of metal and hope. Hour after hour, bolts were loosened and pipes were drained. By the time the new gleaming pump was installed, we had been awake for nearly 24 hours straight. Everyone's faces were glazed with exhaustion. "Start it," I said, praying the machine gods would show mercy. The motor whirred, the pressure gauge flickered… and then nothing. The mill didn't move. The silence that followed was unbearable. You could hear sighs around the room as loud as an October hurricane.

That was the moment I felt something break but inside me. Weeks of effort, nights without sleep, and now this failure. I leaned against the railing, staring blankly at the dead system, feeling the weight of every expectation collapsing. Then came the blow I didn't expect. My engineer walked up, hesitating. "Sir… there's something you should know. The pump we installed... uh… it was stored in the old warehouse. It was declared faulty ten years ago." I blinked, trying to process the words. "Declared faulty? Ten years ago? You mean we just replaced a failed pump with another failed pump?" He nodded, voice barely audible. "Yes, sir. It was tagged as 'not in use' but looked fine, so we tried it." For a moment, my mind went white. One crore rupees' worth of equipment, one day of manpower, and the entire plant down, all because of one wrong assumption. My voice rose for the first time in months. "You knew it was condemned, and you still fitted it?" The engineer's head dropped. The team looked away.

No one spoke. The air felt heavy with regret. I sat down on a stool, defeated. The plant's noise seemed far away. My fitter, Mr. George, sat near me, rubbing his eyes. We didn't speak for a while. Everyone was too tired to be angry anymore.

And then, from somewhere in the fog of fatigue, a thought sparked. "George," I said quietly, "what if it's not the main pump?" He looked at me, confused. "Then what else could it be?" "The pilot pump," I said. He frowned. "The small one mounted on the main pump?" "Yes. If that fails, the swash plate won't move. The main pump won't build pressure." He looked sceptical. "But how do we check that?" "Bring a hydraulic jack, motorized one. We'll see if the swash plate moves." He sighed but nodded. By now, we had nothing left to lose.

At midnight, we dragged the motorized hydraulic jack from the workshop. We set up the test under floodlights. We connected the jack, switched it on, and waited. Nothing happened. For hours, we checked connections, adjusted valves, wiped grease off our eyes. Time blurred. At 4 a.m., the swash plate finally moved, a small, almost invisible motion, but enough to tell us everything. George looked up, eyes wide. "Sir… that means…" "Yes," I said, smiling for the first time in four days. "The pilot pump's dead."

The real culprit wasn't the grand, million-rupee pump we'd blamed. It was a tiny pilot pump worth four thousand rupees. No one no one had paid attention to it as it was buried in the shadows of bigger machinery. For a second, we just stared at each other, too stunned to react. Then laughter broke out, first a chuckle, then uncontrollable fits. It was the laughter of madness, relief, and exhaustion all tangled together. I laughed until tears rolled down my face. George laughed too, wiping his hands on his shirt. Even Mr. Vinayak, who had been standing silently in the background, joined in, shaking his head. "All these cute little pilot pumps," he said between laughs, "haunting us not for days but for ten years." The entire team collapsed into chairs, laughing like lunatics in an oil-soaked comedy. By dawn, we had replaced the tiny pump, refilled the oil, and restarted the system. The pressure gauge rose smoothly. The mill began to turn steadily. It was like watching life return to a body after a long coma. As the sun rose over the plant, the yellow light hit the pipes and metal like a gentle apology. We stood there, greasy, sleepless, but proud.

When the Raw Mill finally began to hum again, the sound of the running plant was almost meditative. The vibration of the floor, the soft hiss of hydraulic lines, the rhythmic turn of the rollers, it all sounded like a lullaby. The team dispersed slowly, one by one. Some went for breakfast, some for sleep, some simply wandered out into the morning light like ghosts returning from a long night. I stayed back a little longer, standing near the pump that had nearly broken us. The tiny innocent pilot pump sat there, unaware of the chaos it had caused. I wanted to pat it on the head and say, "You've been quite the little villain." It struck me how predictable human nature is. The big pump had our full attention, its cost, its size, its reputation. Everyone looked at it, blamed it, and prayed to it. The smaller component went unnoticed.

In that moment, I thought of something I'd once read in The Courage to Be Disliked: that most of our suffering comes from trying to control what isn't really ours to control, while neglecting the small, essential things that actually are. That was exactly what we had done. We had been obsessed with the grand, dramatic failure, the big machine, the big cost, the big spectacle, while the truth was hidden in a humble, neglected detail. It wasn't the main pump that had betrayed us; it was our own blindness to the small. And isn't that how life works too? We chase big promotions, big numbers, big recognitions, all while believing they'll fix everything. But often, what fails us are the tiny pilot pumps of daily life: a conversation we never had, a health check we postponed, a moment of rest we denied ourselves. The small things, ignored long enough, stop the whole system.

I sat down on a toolbox, watching the sunlight creep over the floor. Mr. George was cleaning tools nearby, still humming from relief. Mr. Vinayak walked over, holding a paper cup of tea. "Can't believe it," he said. "Four thousand rupees caused four days of chaos." I smiled. "That's what they call return on investment." He laughed softly. "True. But you know, this incident should go in the plant's history. The day a tiny pump taught us humility." He was right. In those four days, the plant had tested not just our knowledge, but our patience, our endurance, and our ego. We had learned more from failure than from a hundred trainings. Later that evening, after finally catching a few hours of sleep, I walked to the colony garden running the whole incident in my mind again. The pilot pump had come to remind me: that control is an illusion, and humility is the only real skill in engineering — or life. Never underestimate small things. The world falls apart not because of one big mistake, but because of many small ones ignored.

That week, I reread parts of The Courage to Be Disliked. Another line stood out this time: "Courage is not the absence of fear. It's the decision to be disliked for doing what you believe is right." I thought back to those tense hours when everyone doubted my call to test the pilot pump. Logic said it was pointless. But instinct said otherwise. If I'd worried about what others thought, we'd still be sitting there with the wrong pump and the same dead mill. A week later, the incident was formally closed in reports, but informally, it stayed alive in conversations. Engineers joked about it over tea: "Beware of the four-thousand-rupee pilot pumps." Managers used it as an example during audits. And I, well, I carried it as a reminder tucked neatly in my mental toolkit. Whenever new challenges came, I'd think of that night. The image of that small, innocent pump would appear in my mind, as if whispering, "Look at me, I need your attention." Looking back, the incident now feels almost poetic. The plant that prided itself on its massive machines was rescued by the smallest of parts. The engineer who feared failure learned to laugh at it. The team that spent days in tension ended the story with laughter echoing through the Raw Mill building at four in the morning. Sometimes, what saves a machine worth one crore is a four-thousand-rupee pump.

Chapter 7
From Chaos to Crackers to Bell Curve

Every KPI on the dashboard had gone off track.

- The cost of production was climbing.
- Reliability had fallen to an embarrassing level.
- Power consumption graphs were rising every week.
- Plant stoppages filled the calendar without space to breathe.

The review meetings were repetitive. The same questions, the same helpless answers. "What is the plan to control power cost?" "When will reliability improve?" "How long will you need to stabilize?" We had no solid answers left. The team was exhausted. People stopped taking weekly offs. Even Sundays had the same noise as weekdays. Everyone was available all the time and yet nothing was under control. Work had eaten everything. The more we tried to fix things, the worse they seemed to get. Every breakdown solved today reappeared somewhere else tomorrow. Preventive actions were rushed; root-cause analyses ended with temporary answers. We were trapped in short-term fire-fighting. Each day started as a reaction to yesterday's failure. There was no foresight left. No long view. I was living shift to shift, chasing emergencies. Meanwhile, senior management's patience was running out. Warnings became frequent and sharp. Suspension and replacement were openly discussed. The message was clear: fix it or face consequences.

That night, sitting in the control room, I stared at the display screen. The blinking lights felt like a silent reminder that the machines were dictating my routine. The more I chased stability, the more fragile it became. Even at home, I found myself half-listening to family and half-thinking about what might fail next. My sense of leadership was shrinking. I was no longer deciding things; I was only responding. I remember one evening when I returned home after a 20-hour shift. My daughter ran to me, holding her drawing book. I looked at it but couldn't process what she had drawn. My mind was still at the plant. She kept talking; I nodded without hearing. That moment hurt more than the day's failures. I was beginning to lose more than just control over the plant - I was losing presence in my own life.

During one meeting, our VP said coldly, "We can't keep giving excuses. The problems are chronic, but the board wants results. Do whatever it takes." That phrase "whatever it takes" haunted me for weeks. There was no definition to what it meant. It could mean a range of things that I was not sure how to deal with at the point. The next few weeks were relentless. Day shifts blended into nights. Phone calls followed me everywhere. Once, my phone rang while I was in a grocery shop. I left the basket mid-aisle and rushed back to the plant. The call turned out to be minor, but the habit of panic had already set in.

At some point, I realised my decisions were no longer thoughtful, they were reactive. I was saying yes to every request, approving every demand, just to keep things moving. It wasn't leadership; it was survival. I wasn't able to plan properly. I was just empty. That's when it struck me, somewhere along the way, I had stopped leading the plant. The plant was leading me. It was a strange kind of captivity that had no chains or bars, but just endless, mindless responsibility with no finish line. The hardest part was realising that my team looked to me for calm. But I had none left to give. Something had to change, or we would all collapse under the weight of it all. At that point, I didn't know how the turnaround would begin. All I knew was that exhaustion had reached its limit.

It happened one night when the lubrication system alarm went off at 2 a.m. We reached the spot half asleep, expecting a failed pump or a seized bearing. Instead, the entire system was blowing air. Literally. A technician had accidentally connected the air line to the oil inlet. The result was a fountain of oil spraying across the floor. At 3 a.m., covered in oil, standing in that mess, I caught my reflection in the metal surface, shirt sticking to my back, gloves soaked, face black with grime, and couldn't control my laughter. It was the most ridiculous moment of my career. That laughter spread. Others joined and the tension vanished. We cleaned up, fixed the line, and restarted the system by dawn. That small shift, from panic, to acceptance, to even finding humour in the situation, was real progress for the team. Even our VP, who had a reputation for strictness, couldn't escape our collective sense of humour. During a plant visit, his white helmet got splashed with wet cement slurry. He wiped it calmly, looked at us, and said, "Now I look like I belong here." For the first time, everyone laughed in front of him without fear. Moments like these mattered a lot. Because even if they didn't fix machines, they fixed morale. At times, I wondered how our sanity survived those months. I think it was because we learned to find comedy in tragedy. Every disaster carried a lesson, but also a funny story worth telling. When I look back now, I realise that was our turning point. We didn't solve the technical crisis yet, but the mental one had started to ease.

Amid those fatigue-filled days, one morning my wife asked, "When were you last home for an entire day?" I had no answer. Hence, that day, without much thought, I decided to step away for a while. I informed my boss I'd be unavailable for a day. He said nothing for a few seconds, then simply said yes. We went out as a family. A small farmhouse near the city, a pool, some comfort food, a quiet afternoon. No alarms, no calls, no charts. It sounds ordinary, but that one day felt like breathing after months underwater. We swam, ate together, had mocktails, laughed, and did absolutely nothing "useful." For the first time in a long while, I saw my family without the background noise of the plant. I recalled something I had once read in Diary of a CEO by Steven Bartlett. The book talks about the importance of creating space in a leader's mind, space that cannot exist when you are buried under constant noise. When every minute is consumed by calls, alarms, and decisions, you lose the ability to see what actually matters. Bartlett's point was simple: stepping back is not withdrawal, and it is not weakness. It is a deliberate pause that allows you to return with a clearer head and a sharper view of the few issues that can shift everything else. He calls them leverage points; solve those, and half the other problems lose their strength. That idea made complete sense now. I had been drowning in activity, jumping from one crisis to the next, without ever stopping long enough to see the pattern behind them.

So next morning as I stepped into the plant, I called my team together. "We can't solve everything at once," I told them. "Let's pick one issue at a time. Fix it completely. Then move to the next." There was silence in the room. "We are not short of talent," I said. "We are short of focus. Let's assign clear ownership; one person, one priority."

The change didn't happen overnight. It took two full years of steady, disciplined work. One issue at a time, one section at a time. There was no miracle or instant transformation. What shifted was our approach. We stopped jumping from problem to problem and began closing issues completely before moving forward. Each recurring breakdown was mapped, ownership was defined, and follow-ups became routine instead of reactions. Meetings moved from panic-driven discussions to structured reviews. A few chronic failures were eliminated permanently after years of neglect. Power consumption started stabilizing once we removed leakages, corrected settings, and disciplined our operating practices. Preventive maintenance, which earlier felt like a formality, became a real checklist. Fitters and engineers started preparing before shutdowns instead of improvising during them. Within months, patterns emerged. Within a year, we could predict 70% of what was going to fail. Within two years, those predictions reduced because the failures themselves reduced. The control room atmosphere changed and the tension in voices reduced. Then the field changed. You could see it in the way the teams worked in a more coordinate way. Before, five people would stand around a breakdown trying to guess the cause. Now two or three were enough, because they knew exactly what they were looking for. We also became sharper with decisions. Instead of reacting to symptoms, we looked for the systems behind them. Fear was replaced with confidence. Pressure was replaced with responsibility. When senior management asked tough questions, we finally had answers that weren't guesses. And more importantly, those answers translated into results. And so, the team began trusting itself. As reliability improved, production rose. As production rose, the pressure reduced. And as pressure reduced, the team rediscovered its energy. Whenever someone asked how I was managing four lines at once, I gave the same answer: my team. It wasn't modesty. It was the truth. No single person could manage that kind of workload. What made the difference was the collective rhythm that had formed. Everyone knew their scope. Everyone knew the priority.

At home, one evening, my younger daughter sat beside me playing with pop-up crackers. She threw them on the floor and laughed each time they burst. Watching her, I realised how familiar that joy felt. Those little bursts were exactly like the wins we had been creating at work, small actions with big impact. That became my metaphor for leadership: the cracker effect.

When we addressed small chronic issues, the ones everyone ignored because they seemed minor, they exploded into visible results. We fixed a few worn-out couplings that had been running out of alignment for years. The vibration levels dropped. We cleaned oil filters that had never been replaced on time. We started tracking power losses due to compressed air leaks. A few corrections saved lakhs of rupees. We also began recognising people differently. Instead of rewarding only major projects, we started appreciating smaller contributions. A fitter who suggested a design tweak, a shift engineer who caught a deviation early, a helper who noticed an oil leak before it turned into a breakdown, all got public recognition. Those acknowledgments were short, sometimes just a few words of appreciation, but they created pride. People worked better when they knew they were seen. The culture slowly changed. During weekly reviews, I didn't have to push discussions; the team itself brought solutions. The transformation was visible not just in results but in behaviour. People proactively debated, argued, but stayed engaged. The blame game had disappeared. Even management noticed. Our unit, once known for frequent stoppages, started setting new records.

And then yet again, came appraisal season. The timing couldn't have been worse. We had just come out of a difficult phase. Everyone had worked hard, and I knew how much each person had sacrificed. Eighteen engineers reported to me. Every one of them had stayed nights, skipped festivals, and handled pressure without complaint. I remembered that Diwali when Amit sat in the control room while his children were bursting crackers at home. So when HR sent the message about the annual bell curve, I felt uneasy. The curve required that some people must be rated low, no matter how the team performed. I knew what it meant in reality. Even if everyone worked well, someone had to be marked as "below expectation" to fit the shape. It felt wrong. During calibration meetings, HR would share a slide with the neat symmetrical curve, as if human performance naturally distributed itself like height or weight. The HR representative explained it logically: "The bell curve ensures differentiation. Not everyone can be top performer." I understood the theory. But in reality, the curve didn't care whether a person had sacrificed weekends, or handled major breakdowns alone at night, or taught juniors patiently without being asked. According to the bell curve, there must always be tails; people at the bottom even if everyone had delivered well. There must always be a decline, even if the year had been one of collective grit. That was the uncomfortable irony: the better the team performed together, the harder it became to justify pushing someone down.

How could I reduce a year of that to a forced number? That thought disturbed me more than any breakdown ever had. Still, the process had to be completed. The same week, we received appreciation from management for consistent reliability. We had finally brought down stoppages by nearly half. The team deserved celebration. Instead, they got evaluation forms. I remember sitting with the first set of appraisals late at night, surrounded by data and memories. Every rating felt like judgment. For each name, I remembered a moment: someone standing in oil at midnight, someone working through fever, someone missing a family event. Behind every rating was a human story. And yet, the system demanded numbers.

Even now, when performance appraisal season comes around anywhere in the industry, I feel a familiar tug in my stomach. It is a strange mixture of half amusement and half discomfort because I have lived both sides of that process. Some people think appraisals are merely administrative cycles. For those who sit on the other side of the table, the ones who rate, it feels something heavier. You are not judging numbers; you are judging effort, circumstances, behaviour, growth, and character. But the system wants it simple. It wants a bell curve. There is no column titled "personal sacrifice." There is no weightage for emotional resilience. A bell curve does not feel the heartbeat behind performance. Still, we followed it blindly like a doctrine. I often wished I could tear the chart apart and declare, "Everyone gets what they have earned." But leadership is rarely that simple. You work within the boundaries given, and within those boundaries, you must still find a way to be fair.

That's when I decided to approach it differently. I stopped rating performances from memory. Memory is biased by recent events. Instead, I tracked habits - consistency, sincerity, reliability, ownership. I asked myself one question for every engineer: "Did this person perform honestly?" If the answer was yes, he got the rating he deserved. If he went beyond, took initiative, solved a chronic issue, trained others, I marked him higher. It didn't fit the perfect curve, but it fit my conscience. When the review session ended, HR politely reminded me that the curve still needed to balance. I adjusted only what was absolutely necessary but refused to reduce anyone unfairly. That year, our section's results were among the best. We broke production records and won recognition for reliability improvement. The irony wasn't lost on me: the same team that the bell curve would have divided had lifted the plant together. In that moment, I understood leadership in a new way. It isn't about following systems blindly. It's about protecting people from systems when they stop making sense.

Some people questioned why I rated certain engineers higher when their failures were also visible. My answer was simple: the rating reflected not just results but the intent and honesty behind them. Machines fail for many reasons; design flaws, age, wrong spares, delayed approvals, or even poor historical decisions that no one currently on the team was responsible for. Should one engineer bear the punishment for a decade-old choice he never made? So I rated as fairly as I could, bending the curve where necessary but not breaking my conscience in the process. Even then, the guilt never fully went away. The bell curve taught me something unexpected: a leader cannot control the system, but he can control how humanely he uses it.

Chapter 8
From Stents to Strategy

The surgical lights at Mewar Hospital have a peculiar interrogative personality. The moment they flashed above me, I felt like a suspect who had been caught red-handed for a crime I didn't remember committing.

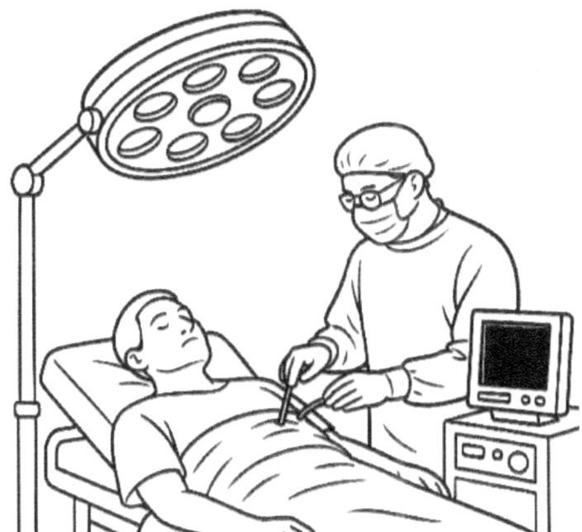

One minute I was dealing with bell curves and corporate contradictions, the next minute I was lying on a hospital bed with a cannula taped to my hand, preparing for yet another laparoscopy on my left ureter. It was my third time under those lights. Even the anaesthetist recognized me by now. "Back again?" he asked casually, as if I had simply returned to exchange a shirt. I smiled weakly. "If you guys had a loyalty card, I would have earned a free cappuccino by now." He chuckled, then placed the mask on my face. As the world blurred into soft edges, I thought about the absurdity of it all; how a body that had survived breakdowns, shutdowns, and boardroom fireworks could be crippled by a mineral the size of a grain of sand. The procedure was routine. Too routine by now. Stent insertion, stone removal, standard laparoscopic finesse. When I woke up, the lights had stopped interrogating me. Instead, the dull, familiar pain returned, hugging my lower abdomen like an unwelcome relative. A nurse approached. "Successful surgery. Please rest as much as you can." Rest! A beautiful concept! Like unicorns, world peace, and honest appraisals. I nodded.

The week crawled by with a mix of painkillers, metallic-tasting meals, and slow walks. When the day arrived to remove the stent, I entered the procedure room. "Done," the doctor declared after a few minutes, as if he had simply unplugged a USB drive.I walked out believing that the episode was over. It wasn't. Life, I've learned, rarely wraps up its lessons neatly. Especially when it wants to test the sturdiness of your character. Or in this case, your ureter. The nightmare returned within days. A sharp, stabbing pain hit my left flank. I bent over instinctively, clutching my side, gasping for breath. The urine flow slowed to a miserable trickle, then stopped completely. My body went into panic mode, and I staggered toward the car, holding onto the railing like a climber gripping the last edge of a cliff. The emergency room welcomed me like a loyal old friend. Another scan. Another round of sympathetic head shakes. Another surgical discussion that sounded like déjà vu. "The stone has slipped and blocked the ureter again." Of course it had. I signed the consent form and back into the OT I went, revisiting the same fluorescent ceiling, the same cold table, the same routine. My internal monologue tried to keep things light: Dear hospital, please issue me a season pass. Call it "Surgery Unlimited." Somewhere between the injections and the dull throb of stitched flesh, I remembered a line from HBR's Essentials on Resilience. They called such events "crucibles of leadership." Leadership? At that moment, I felt less like iron being forged and more like bread being roasted. Pain, that relentless professor, was teaching me patience. I didn't feel strong then. I didn't feel wise. But leadership, I would later learn, is shaped in pain and tested in silence.

Leaving the hospital and returning to the plant felt like switching from a silent monastery to a bustling village fair. My body felt like it still carried traces of anaesthesia, suppressed pain, and the emotional residue of too many fluorescent ceilings. But the plant had no mercy. In fact it was waiting for me was the industrial equivalent of an endurance marathon: a 4-line shutdown. Shutdowns are not maintenance events. They are mechanical Kumbh Melas, thousands of people, hundreds of tasks, and infinite chaos. Planning for this shutdown had begun nine months earlier, back in December. Like delivering an industrial baby, minus the celebration and with significantly more paperwork.

Those December days came back to me in fragments. I remembered the first bar chart we made, a giant rectangular beast with tightly packed rows and columns. Each bar represented a job: conveyor overhaul, pump replacement, duct modifications, lubrication line rerouting, refractory patching, pulley lagging, alignment, calibration, an orchestra of activities with budgets and timelines. Contractors were summoned like armies before a war. Their scopes were explained, diagrams drawn, execution windows finalized, and safety protocols handed over like sacred scriptures. Then came the Purchase Requests (PRs). In theory, PRs are simple. In practice, they behave like migratory birds; you send them out and wait endlessly for them to return. They need signatures, approvals, budget checks, vendor quotes, re-verification, clarifications, and sometimes an office puja for good luck. Once PRs are approved, they transform into Purchase Orders (POs). If PRs are migratory birds, POs are teenage hippies on a road trip. You must chase them like a CRM tool with legs. Buyers, in turn, chase vendors. Vendors chase transporters. Transporters chase the idea of punctuality. And somewhere in this relay race, you lose the energy to chase your own meals.

One of the biggest battles was with OEM service engineers. You had to book them months in advance, arrange travel, coordinate guest house rooms, confirm airport pickups, and pray they didn't receive an emergency call from another plant. I sometimes wondered whether I was managing a shutdown or a five-star hospitality conference. My job description unofficially expanded to: Shutdown Hospitality Manager, Concierge-in-Chief, and Emotional Counsellor for Contractors. Manpower planning was also a huge chunk of it. Welders, fitters, riggers, helpers, gas cutters, each category needed precise allocation. If even one welder went missing, half the schedule got derailed. Heavy equipment like cranes, trailers and hydras had to be lined up in perfect harmony. Temporary facilities for resting, drinking water and food were arranged like a small city. On some days, I felt I was building a wedding pavilion rather than a maintenance camp. Safety documents were stacking up on my desk: HIRAs (Hazard Identification and Risk Assessments), SWPs (Safe Work Procedures), work permits, job safety analyses to name a few. I could recite most of them from memory. Before work began each morning, I'd run through the safety briefing with contractors. By the end, I'd hand them stapled papers and say, "Acknowledgement here, please," like a celebrity distributing autographs. One contractor once asked softly, "Sir, can I get your signature too?" I replied, "If you finish your work on time, I'll even give you my PAN number." Shutdown humour, like shutdown manpower, appeared from strange corners.

In the middle of all this, I often reread Blue Ocean Strategy. The book served as my mental detox. While the plant swirled in red-ocean chaos of too many jobs, too many teams, too few welding points, I needed a blue-ocean mind-set. So I created my own shutdown ocean. Contractor clashes? Eliminated through clear time slots. Resource fights? Avoided by establishing a master coordination board. Welding point shortages? Resolved by allocating zones. Workmen fatigue? Reduced with scheduled breaks and food stalls. Safety violations?

Minimized through real-time monitoring. Slowly, instead of reacting to chaos, I was designing systems. That was my plan to transform the shutdown to an ecosystem.

But planning can only take you so far. When the shutdown actually started, the entire plant transformed into a mechanical carnival. Hydras nudged trailers. Gas cylinders hissed. Scaffolding teams climbed like human monkeys. Welding sparks flew like Diwali before schedule. The smell of grease, steel, paint, and dust blended into a signature aroma that only cement engineers can acknowledge and appreciate. Every hour was an exam. Every job, a ticking clock. Every delay, a minor heart attack.

At 3 a.m., when exhaustion crept like a silent intruder, humour was my fuel. I'd tell the team: "Shutdown planning is like wedding planning. No matter how perfectly you prepare, someone will still complain, 'the dessert was too sweet?'" Or "Guest house staff thinks I'm running a tour package: Welcome to Shutdown City, full boarding included." Sometimes the laughter was real. Sometimes it was just a release valve for collective stress. But it always helped.

By the end of the shutdown, the plant looked renewed. Standing in the dust, leaning on a railing, inhaling the scent of hot metal, I felt a rare satisfaction. My hospital scars had healed enough for me to forget the pain. But the shutdown scars, those invisible ones of leadership, pressure, and strategy, those stayed throughout my life. Shutdowns had taught me more than any management course ever could. I didn't earn an MBA. But somewhere between stents and schedules, I earned competence.

Shutdown fatigue has a unique aftertaste. It's a blend of accomplishment and accumulated exhaustion; something between the satisfaction of climbing a mountain and the numbness of realizing you still have to climb back down. The only thing scarier than a shutdown is a shutdown inspection. And the only thing scarier than a shutdown inspection is a shutdown inspection by Mr. Sunny. In our cluster, Mr. Sunny's name didn't need introduction; it needed dosage instructions. He had a reputation for thoroughness. The man would check a machine like a surgeon examining an organ before transplant. The day arrived with little ceremony but with significant tension. Mr. Sunny walked into the plant without coffee, greetings, or warming-up conversation. "Let's go," he said. We began at the ground floor. He moved methodically, scanning every surface with the kind of silent concentration usually reserved for bomb squad technicians. Then he

started climbing. And climbing. And climbing. If shutdown was my MBA, this inspection felt like the fitness test for the graduation ceremony. At level after level, he checked motors, ducts, fasteners, alignment, welding quality, oil levels, and the reliability of every component we had touched in the past two weeks. He asked precise questions, the kind that makes you realize whether you have actually mastered your job or were merely playing confident. His eyes scanned the environment with a practiced rhythm. The climb continued until we reached the eighth floor. At that height, something inexplicable happens inside your body - your lungs negotiate with your pride, and most people surrender. Not Mr. Sunny. He walked across the platform casually and pointed at a flange. “This weld looks superior. Who did it?” “Contractor Bansal’s team,” I said, trying not to pant. “Good. Keep them in priority next time.” Such sentences were the equivalent of blessings in our industrial universe. We all gathered around on the platform for a few minutes. Tea at 130 meters height, wind brushing our faces, the sunlight casting long shadows across the plant, it felt surreal. Shutdowns rarely give you moments that feel human. This was one of them. I still remember how we laughed at a small joke someone cracked about how preheater floors should have escalators. Someone suggested taking a selfie. There we stood: Shutdown team, exhausted but proud. Machines shining. And Mr. Sunny in the centre, helmet tilted slightly, expression composed, eyes softened. Click. A tiny moment in the middle of mechanical chaos. A picture we would all later show our families.

By the end of the round, Mr. Sunny looked at me and said: "You've done solid preparation. Your team has worked hard. Good job." In corporate language, that sentence may sound ordinary. In shutdown language, it is poetry. Very few people understand the emotional lift such words bring to an engineer. We don't crave applause on stages. Our medals are functioning machines. Our trophies are well-executed shutdowns. Later in the evening, when the team gathered near the canteen, everyone looked revitalized and happy. But beneath that, a truth stood firm: Only we knew the sleepless nights we had spent. Only we knew the chaos we had wrestled. Only we knew the effort behind each repaired component. And for once, someone else, someone who mattered, had seen it too. That tea break at 130 meters remained a bookmark in my memory. In HBR terms, this was the moment when performance became visible performance.

After the shutdown and after surviving Mr. Sunny's altitudinal test of character, I believed I had earned a brief pause. But corporate life has a sense of timing that rivals slapstick comedy. Just when your shoulders finally drop, a new announcement appears, ready to drag them back up. For me, that announcement came as a phone call from HR. "Shahbaz, please come to the office. It's regarding the General Manager position." My stomach reacted faster than my brain. Some people experience butterflies when excited. Mine was a whole aviary of nervous pigeons trying to escape through my ribs. I was given an opportunity yet again. An interview for GM, where the panel consisted of Unit Heads, Presidents,

Senior Vice Presidents, and a few other sharp-eyed gentlemen. So for the first time since I started my plant life, I decided to prepare with the intensity of a board student. So I started spending time with managers and operators of other departments whenever I could.

I started with the Quality Control (QC) department. QC experts have a natural gift for speaking in numbers and charts the way poets speak in metaphors. They explained clinker quality, Blaine fineness, residue validation, gypsum dehydration curves, and the emotional instability of C3S. I filled pages of my notebook with their insights, which now looked like mathematical graffiti. Then I moved to the Central Control Room (CCR). CCR operators are the pilots of a cement plant; eyes glued to the DCS screens and ears trained to detect anomalies before alarms even beep. They showed me kiln parameters, raw mill loads, cyclone efficiency patterns, reasons for erratic draft, and the mysterious mood swings of the cooler. One of them pointed at a trend line and said, “Sir, see this? This dip? I knew something was wrong and boom! The alarm went off.” Next came mechanical, electrical, instrumentation, AFR, packing plant, and logistics. I sat with each team, trying to absorb as much know-how as I could. The more I studied, the more my confidence grew. HBR describes the “confidence-competence loop: the more you learn, the more confident you feel. The more confident you feel, the more effectively you learn.”

The day of the interview arrived. I wore a crisp shirt, polished shoes, and a mask of composure. On the inside, the pigeons in my stomach were still flapping.

The boardroom felt like an amphitheatre of judgment. A long table. Ten chairs. Ten faces. Ten different styles of evaluation. Some smiled. Some had stern faces. Some merely observed, like hawks assessing a movement in the grass. The Unit Head began. "So, Shahbaz. Tell us about you and your journey in the field so far." I summarized my journey by highlighting the years spent handling breakdowns, shutdowns, raw mill challenges, and night inspections that shaped my practical understanding of the plant. When the panel evaluated my technical depth, I explained reliability management through vibration root-cause analysis, alignment accuracy, and preventive discipline; managing preheater draft by monitoring cyclone health, fan behavior, and leakages; resolving cross-functional issues through empathy, involvement, and clarity; optimizing shutdowns through structured planning; and reducing overall costs by focusing on energy efficiency, resource utilization, and a preventive culture. When I spoke, I realized every word came from hands-on experience, not from notebooks. In fact, the more I spoke, the more confident I felt. And the more they listened, the more present I became.

Somewhere on between, the President leaned forward. "What do you think makes you ready for this role?" A dangerous question. A revealing question. I took a breath and replied, "Sir, I've worked in plants where breakdowns dictated life. I've worked in plants where shutdowns felt like wars. I've worked with people who came from different worlds. I've learned to make decisions when data was incomplete and pressure was complete. I've learned to lead with patience because I have realized machines don't respond to aggression and people don't respond to fear. I've learned that reliability is all about mind-set. And I've learned that strategy is useless without execution." Silence. Then slow nods.

The interview ended with a few formalities. As I stood up, the SVP said: "Good. Very good." Those three words held more relief than pain-killers after surgery. I walked out feeling satisfied. After some time, the HR called "Congratulations, Shahbaz. You're selected." For a few seconds, I stared at the wall. My whole career flashed before my eyes. From shutdown trenches to the boardroom table, the journey had taken everything, sweat, blood, cement and steel. Now it had brought me here. To this moment. It felt surreal that the same young man who started his career in a three-seated hostel room, was now standing at the doorstep of becoming a General Manager. I remembered those nights clearly: the 2 a.m. breakdown calls, the cold mess food, the fatigue that sat inside my bones, and the anxiety that clung to my pillow. I had no roadmap, no privilege, no confidence. All I had was relentless determination and a willingness to pick myself up after every failure.

My sacrifices flashed through my mind with uncomfortable clarity. How many times had I told my parents, "I'll come next month," and that next month never came? My daughter grew, my parents aged, and I kept telling myself it was temporary. My wife carried responsibilities I should have shared, but my world revolved around shutdowns, breakdowns, and production targets. My health paid its own price, sleepless nights, skipped meals, stress-induced spikes, surgeries, the stents, the hospital lights. I gave the plant more time than I ever gave myself. And yet, machines turned out to be the most honest teachers I ever had. They broke down without warning, forcing me to learn patience. They refused to run until every detail was respected, teaching me discipline. They punished shortcuts and rewarded effort, shaping my technical instincts more than any textbook ever could. Every vibration, every draft change, every stubborn bearing carved lessons deeper than classroom theory ever would.

Through all of this, my team has been my backbone. They stayed awake when I stayed awake, worked through fatigue when I worked through fatigue, stood with me in every crisis. Whatever strength I carried into that interview room was a reflection of them. Now, as I stand on the verge of becoming GM, I know the title isn't a reward, it's a responsibility. Leadership will test me in new ways, not through machines this time but through people, trust, and decisions that shape futures. The journey was not easy, but it has prepared me to lead with humility and resilience.

Chapter 9
Builders, Fighters, & Escapers

I never thought I would own a car in my life. When I first joined the manufacturing world, I was the kind of person who thought "four wheels" meant factory trolleys and kiln shells, not personal vehicles. A car felt like one of those distant luxuries meant for people with predictable work hours, tidy white-collar jobs, and a linear career graph. Much later, when I read Jim Collins' Good to Great, I found the perfect metaphor for my journey: the flywheel. Collins writes about how giant wheels don't start spinning because of one big push, but they accelerate through many small pushes over time. Each invisible effort adds weight, adds motion, adds momentum. And then the wheel begins to turn on its own. My car key, years later, is the physical symbol of that flywheel. factory was where this invisible wheel began its slow, stubborn rotation.

Alpha wasn't just a workplace; it was an initiation ceremony. It stripped your illusion of control, peeled away your textbook theories, and trained you in the raw, unfiltered language of machines. It introduced me to personalities that would later become case studies in my mind for both inspiration and confusion. The plant itself was an organism. On humid days, motors would groan more loudly. On cold nights, bearings would stiffen like old men with knee pain. And the smell! Oh, the smell! A signature perfume of warm cement dust mixed with hydraulic oil. There was something else about Alpha which I didn't appreciate initially but later understood. Alpha gave me exposure to variety. Big plants of taught me chaos: multiple lines, hundreds of machines, endless energy and the thrill of solving three problems simultaneously while four new ones appear magically. Small plants taught me precision: strict routines, lean manpower, tight control, and the unforgiving reality that even the smallest mistake could become visible immediately. Alpha gave me both. And then, Alpha gave me the people.

The first personality was Mr. Sunny. He had a talent for frightening people without raising his voice. Suspension and termination were just tools for him. He believed in strong discipline, strict accountability, and a management style so direct it could slice through concrete. And the one person who got caught in this storm unfairly was my subordinate Rajeev. Rajeev was a good performer. He followed instructions, delivered output, and rarely created drama. The first time Sunny visited the plant, Rajeev became a scapegoat for issues far bigger than him. Nobody planned it, but these things happen in manufacturing. It shook him deeply. Pressure, yes, but this was fear coated with uncertainty. Rajeev began looking for another job the same evening. By the second visit, Sunny had spoken sharply to him again, and that was enough. Rajeev resigned and left quietly. I didn't blame him. Not everyone is built for unpredictability. Rajeev was not an Escaper because he was weak; he was an Escaper because he valued peace more than confrontation. And peace is a valid goal. On the opposite end of the spectrum was my AFR subordinate, a man who did not run from pressure but combusted inside it. He was the kind of engineer who thought diplomacy was a conspiracy. He spoke bluntly in meetings, corrected seniors mid-sentence, argued over trivial things, and delivered feedback like he was firing bullets. He believed honesty meant volume, and transparency meant aggression. Where Rajeev saw fear, he saw war. Meetings with him were unforgettable experiences. For a while, his aggression worked. In manufacturing, sometimes raw force gets short-term results. But in the long run, aggression without emotional calibration is like running an endless marathon; it collapses eventually. And so did he. His relationships soured. Seniors distanced themselves. Peers avoided him. Even his juniors whispered privately that reporting to him was like "entering a hungry lion's den." Ultimately, he too left. Mind you, it was not because of performance issues, but because his temperament made the environment un-workable. Watching these two, the Escaper and the Fighter, taught me profound lessons. They were like two sides of a leadership coin, both teaching me what not to become.

Then destiny balanced the equation by sending me two Builder archetypes. One was Mr. Vijay, the most cheerful man in a 10-km radius. If factory was a battlefield of machines, tempers, and relentless pressure, then Vijay was the rare soldier who walked through it all with a smile. There was something unmistakably disarming about his presence, an almost childlike sincerity wrapped inside a grown man. While most engineers navigated the plant with nervous shoulders and heavy steps, Vijay moved as though the plant were a beloved playground he had grown up in. He didn't just solve problems; he dissolved their tension. When management handed him charge of four mills simultaneously, the rest of us silently held our breath. Most engineers would have responded with a request for additional manpower, an updated chair with better back support, or at least a day to mentally prepare. Vijay simply grinned, nodded, and asked if he could start immediately. His enthusiasm was so genuine that it made the rest of us wonder whether he knew something about stress that we didn't.

His office reflected his personality, a curious blend of chaos and comfort. While other cabins maintained a strict environment of files, binders, and neat pen stands, Vijay's room resembled a cross between a maintenance workshop, a pantry, and a laughter club. At any moment, he could be found surrounded by workmen, supervisors, contractors, or colleagues, all of whom gravitated toward him. Conversations in his office flowed like rivers. Aroma of chai mixed with the low hum of discussions and occasional bursts of laughter made his cabin feel like the safest corner of the plant. And Vijay never hesitated to ask for help. Many engineers think admitting ignorance reduces their authority. Not Vijay. He walked into peer cabins with the openness of a student visiting a professor. "Explain this part," he would say, resting one elbow on someone's desk, "because your experience will save my time." People rarely refused him. His humility made every person around him feel wiser, and his confidence made them feel trusted. It was a unique charisma.

One incident captures his spirit perfectly. One evening, while handling multiple urgent tasks, he needed an angle grinder. He rushed into a colleague's cabin and asked for it. The colleague, distracted and half-listening, pointed vaguely to a corner and said, "There it is" Vijay grabbed the machine and bolted toward the mill, only to discover that what he held was not an angle grinder but a mixer grinder. Any other engineer would have thrown a fit, stormed back in anger, or at least scolded the colleague for the confusion. Vijay, instead, plugged the mixer into a socket, switched it on dramatically, and declared to the team, "Well, if we can't grind the mill today, we can at least make chutney for the night shift!" The tired, irritated faces around him broke instantly into laughter. That was Vijay's true gift. He recognized that manufacturing isn't just an engineering discipline; it's a psychological battleground. And when you can influence human mood positively, half the battle is won.

But laughter alone doesn't qualify someone as a leader. Vijay paired his light-heartedness with deep sincerity. He took responsibility without hesitation and admitted his mistakes without shame. He never blamed subordinates to save himself, never exaggerated problems to earn sympathy, and never made promises he couldn't keep. His credibility kept growing because his integrity was quietly, consistently present in every interaction.

Where Vijay mastered emotional intelligence, Vinay, my mentor and the "Bheeshm Pitamah of Reliability," mastered technical and strategic clarity. The two men were opposites in personality but identical in impact. If Vijay was the warmth that energized teams, Vinay was the mountain that steadied them. He had an uncanny ability to assess a failing machine the way a seasoned doctor reads a patient's eyes. You brought him a crisis and he returned it to you in solvable fragments. The day the roller crusher shaft disaster struck remains etched in my memory. The flange bolts had sheared off, causing the shaft to fall inside the box. Panic buzzed across the shop floor like electricity through a loose terminal. There were no spares, and the estimated cost of a new shaft was unsettling enough to make even senior leaders visibly tense. Vinay walked in calmly and examined the wreckage. After a few minutes of silent evaluation, he called me over. His voice was gentle but precise. "We'll do two things," he said, almost casually. "First, reduce the shaft length by fifty millimetres and make a tap hole. Second, increase the stub shaft length accordingly." That was it. The repair cost dropped from nearly one crore to seven lakhs, and the shaft worked flawlessly afterward. Senior management praised it widely. But what stayed with me was Vinay's approach. He didn't fight the problem; he understood it. He didn't react emotionally; he responded logically. Brian Tracy wrote that most large problems can be solved by simply identifying the next right step. Vinay took that principle and applied it with surgical precision. Vinay also taught me how to keep myself happy in tough situations. Once, he and I went to get some papers signed. The moment we entered the boss's office, his boss suddenly started screaming and shouting at both of us. We didn't argue, didn't defend, we just nodded, walked out, and the moment we were in the corridor, we both burst into laughter. Vinay whispered, "We are paid for listening to the boss. Might as well enjoy the show!"

By the time my journey at factory reached its natural conclusion, I realized that understanding people was as essential as understanding machines. Every day added another paragraph to a chapter that was still unfolding. I saw a pattern enough to categorize the people around me, not because I wanted to label them, but because the categories helped me understand how different minds responded under the same pressure. I kept seeing the same three archetypes repeat: Escapers, Fighters, and Builders. And each taught me something different, often without knowing it. The Escapers, like Rajeev, showed me the vulnerability that sits beneath competence. I saw how the fear of criticism can overshadow talent. I saw how unpredictability in leadership can slowly drain someone's confidence until leaving feels like the only way to breathe. Rajeev's exit wasn't a failure, his or the plant's. It was a reminder that every workplace contains people who are technically strong but emotionally fragile. Not everyone is built to survive a leadership style that thrives on fear. And that truth made me more thoughtful about how I dealt with my own juniors. If pressure could push someone like

Rajeev out, then perhaps leadership was not about "hardening" people, but about recognizing who needed support and who needed space.

On the opposite end stood the Fighters; strong, capable, and often too sharp for their own good. My AFR subordinate was their ambassador. He fought everything: issues, people, meetings, opinions, instructions. Confrontation was a tool. Honesty was a weapon. And authority was something to challenge rather than respect. While Escapers ran from storms, Fighters ran into them. His departure taught me something the manuals never mention: uncontrolled aggression is another form of fragility. Fighters often leave not because they are defeated, but because they exhaust themselves battling imaginary enemies. His downfall was emotional than technical. And witnessing it made me vow that I would never let competence blind me to the necessity of diplomacy. In the plant, intelligence might open doors, but temperament decides how long you stay inside.

And then came the Builders, the people who neither flee nor fight blindly. They construct. They stabilize. They absorb chaos and return clarity. They don't blame; they don't dramatize; they don't collapse. They simply build. Vijay and Vinay, in different ways, belonged to this rare category, and observing them reshaped my understanding of what leadership truly means. Vijay taught me that the most underrated leadership skill is emotional resilience. He laughed through challenges, made his team feel valued, asked questions openly, and turned confusion into collective brainstorming.

Watching him taught me that morale is not a soft concept, it is an operational asset. A team that feels safe and appreciated works faster, thinks better, and breaks less often. Vinay taught me the power of structured thinking, of breaking problems into solvable fragments, of approaching crises with deliberate calm. His ability to extract simple solutions from complex situations was mastery. And it taught me that in manufacturing, clarity is not just intellectual strength, it is an emotional discipline.

As I continued working at Alpha, these three archetypes appeared everywhere. A new hire would panic like an Escaper. A senior engineer would blast through meetings like a Fighter. A junior technician would surprise me by showing the calm persistence of a Builder. I also observed that people are not static. The same person can shift categories depending on circumstances, leaders, pressures, and even their personal life outside the plant. Escapers can become Builders with the right guidance. Fighters can evolve into Builders when they learn restraint. And Builders, if overloaded for too long, can become Escapers temporarily. This realization also changed the way I judged, the way I delegated, the way I listened, and the way I led. It made me more aware of my own behaviour. Because I wasn't immune to these categories either. There were days I felt like Rajeev, overwhelmed, insecure, afraid of criticism. There were days I felt like the AFR subordinate, angry, impulsive, convinced I was right. But slowly, through every crisis, I tried my best to internalize the qualities of the Builders. Even today one truth resonates with me: Success in the plant is not about escaping or fighting the plant. It is about building yourself strong enough to stand inside it.

Chapter 10
The Great Rake Revolution

When I first joined factory, I thought my professional life would revolve around the comforting predictability of mechanical engineering. I was a mechanical guy. But Paramount had other plans for my career. Slowly, almost mischievously, my job profile expanded into a buffet menu. One week I was troubleshooting electrical drives; the next week I was coordinating with instrumentation; the following month I was sitting in a lab discussing cement fineness; and by the quarter's end, I was arguing with railways about dispatch schedules. If someone had shaken me awake at 3 a.m. and asked, "What is your department?" I would have replied, "The entire plant." It became a running joke that if a meteorite ever hit the factory, the first person they would call would be me, because somehow it would fall under my "extended portfolio." Nothing, however, prepared me for the part of my role that involved dealing with the packing and dispatch team. This team had a ritual. Every morning, without fail, the moment I entered the dispatch office, the team would turn toward me with an expression of resigned certainty and announce, "Sir, only one rake today." It was said with such practiced harmony that sometimes I wondered if they rehearsed it the night before. And as if the script demanded it, I would ask my obligatory question: "But why only one?" Then came the whisper filled with equal parts fear, reverence, and superstition. "DC cost." DC cost, in reality, was a very small penalty paid to the railways if a rake remained idle for too long. It was the financial equivalent of handful peanuts. But if you heard my team speak about it, you'd think DC cost would make the cement companies bankrupt. Their fear was so deep-rooted that it shaped every decision they made. Their lives moved in alignment with the orbit of DC cost. The result of this fear-driven culture was predictable: stagnation. Our dispatch numbers barely moved. Our silos remained overloaded to the brim. The marketing team kept asking for higher dispatch; logistics begged for faster movement; the plant availability was good; the market demand was strong. Everything was aligned except the courage of my dispatch team. They guarded the "one rake system" with the devotion of grandparents guarding their fixed deposit receipts. It was maddening. And yet, every day, the chorus continued: one rake, one rake, one rake.

One morning, after hearing that dreaded line for what felt like the thousandth time, I snapped. Maybe it was the extra-strong tea that had kicked my neurons awake. Maybe it was the boredom of routine. Maybe it was the suffocating certainty that if I didn't break the pattern, nothing would ever change. The team repeated their familiar chant, "Sir, one rake today", and before my logical mind could intervene, I said without hesitation, "Today, we order two rakes." Silence fell instantly.

Cathedral silence. I noticed one person's pen slipped from his fingers and rolled across the table. Another stared at the ceiling as if waiting for divine lightning. Someone close to the door muttered a quick prayer. It was as if I had announced a plan to invade a neighbouring country. Within minutes, my boss summoned me. His face was the perfect blend of shock, irritation, and impending doom. What followed was less a discussion and more a courtroom drama. He dissected my decision from every angle. He asked me if I had any idea what I was doing. He reminded me about DC cost as if I hadn't heard of it since I arrived here. He questioned my judgement, my risk appetite, and possibly even my academic degree. But the irony was that the more he spoke out of fear, the clearer my own mind became. I understood the problem wasn't DC cost; it was psychological paralysis. The problem was inherited fear, passed down from one generation of dispatch staff to another like an unwanted heirloom.

And so, instead of retreating, I took the scariest step possible: I escalated upward. Not out of disrespect, but out of responsibility. I asked for a meeting with my boss's boss. I explained the situation, the habitual fear, the lost opportunity, and the fact that the penalty was negligible compared to the growth we could unlock. He listened quietly. Then he asked a simple question: "What exactly is the DC cost?" When I told him, he almost laughed. Then he leaned back and said, in the calmest voice I had heard in weeks, "Forget the DC cost. It's nothing compared to what we'll gain. Go ahead." And that was it, the moment that broke the myth and the imaginary DC monster poofed into thin air. That very evening, I wrote to the logistics head, Mr. Sandeep, informing him that starting immediately, we would operate with two rakes per day. And thus, a new chapter had begun.

The day after the two-rake announcement was intense. There was a strange hum in the dispatch building. When I walked in, the team looked at me as though I were returning from a dangerous expedition. I pretended not to notice the theatrics. Inside, I felt a mix of adrenaline and calm stubbornness. I had disturbed a comfortable cycle, and people rarely thank you for that on day one.

The two rakes had been arranged; the schedule was locked; the railways had confirmed movement. Now the real question stood like a stern school principal: Could we actually handle it? The first rake rolled in before noon. Production responded well; the packing machines ran steadily; the loading crew worked with mechanical discipline. Everyone held their breath, watching the hours tick past, waiting for the disaster they were certain would arrive. But nothing happened. The rake moved. The wagons filled. The line cleared. And then, unexpectedly, beautifully, the first rake was out on time. But the bigger test was the second rake. It came in during the evening, when the team usually relaxed, mentally signing off from the day's responsibilities. This time, there was no room for relaxation. They straightened their backs. They tightened their grips. No one dared to be casual. That second rake became the turning point. As it approached, I stood on the loading platform with my team. I could sense their fear and reluctance. But when the second rake cleared too, the silence that followed was different. Their fear had transformed to disbelief mixed with the faintest seed of pride.

Yet, not everyone shared the sentiment. That night, my boss called me again. This time, the drama had mellowed. His voice was tired, worried, but strangely gentler. “Are you sure this will work?” he asked. Behind that simple question was an ocean of anxiety. He wasn’t worried about DC cost alone. He was worried about responsibility, his responsibility. If anything went wrong, he would have to answer for it. Fear travels downward quickly, but upward it carries weight. I could sense that the burden on his shoulders was heavier than the one on mine. I assured him calmly and clearly. And I meant it. The big boss had given his blessing. The logic was sound. The opportunity was real. It was a calculated shift in attitude.

The effects of the two-rake experiment had begun to show within a couple of days. The silos, usually swollen with overnight accumulation, were half empty. The packing machines weren’t idling. The dispatch corridor, once a place of lethargic movement, felt like an airport terminal. People walked more efficiently. The whole ecosystem felt alive. I didn’t have to declare anything anymore. When the team gathered for the daily meeting and asked, “Sir… today also two rakes?” the question carried less resistance and more cautious curiosity. It was the first crack in the wall of fear. A week after introducing two rakes, I proposed few more ideas. We experimented with adjusting silo charging patterns and loading schedules. We aligned packing machines in a staggered sequence. We reorganized manpower placement. And then, one calm afternoon, we handled three rakes. The fear that once crippled the department suddenly had no footing. It was astonishing to watch. The same team moved three rakes with the brisk confidence of people who had forgotten they once worshipped a penalty charge. The dispatch building now echoed with words like "optimization," "turnaround," and "parallel loading," phrases that had never previously entered their vocabulary.

The thing is, once success becomes familiar, fear becomes irrelevant. The magic of momentum is that no one notices the exact moment it begins. There is no dramatic announcement, but once a team tastes a minor success, it alters the emotional climate of the room. That's what happened with dispatch. Once the second rake succeeded, the third felt less extraordinary. Once the third worked, the idea of three-and-a-half didn't seem impossible. And once that became a routine, the team even began volunteering ideas. We were achieving 3.5 rakes per day. It was our new normal. The team that once clung to "Sir, one rake only," now asked, "Sir… if market demand supports it, can we attempt four?" And there was no tremble in their voice. It was astonishing to observe how human psychology behaves when fear is removed. For years, DC cost had been a mythical dragon guarding the cave. But once the team discovered the dragon was actually a gecko with a loud reputation, everything changed.

As the transformation unfolded, I noticed the unique personalities around me who contributed to this revolution, each with their own quirks, habits, and leadership styles. These characters were sculptors shaping the outcome. The packing team was the first group I observed with renewed appreciation. For years, they had behaved like financial guardians of the cement world. Risk, to them, was a sin. They approached cement loading with the conservative mindset, even though the company needed bold investments of effort. Yet, beneath their rigid exterior lay an unspoken loyalty. Once convinced, they delivered with overcompensation. Then there was my boss, a man with a passionate heart but a nervous system wired in the tightest way possible. For him, the mere mention of demurrage could induce mild palpitations. He lived with an exaggerated sense of responsibility that made him anxious at any deviation from routine. He feared mistakes not because he lacked capacity, but because he carried accountability like a weighted vest. He would pace up and down the corridor when two rakes were scheduled, shaking his head, muttering under his breath. Only after seeing that the numbers were real and sustainable, his anxiety slowly made space for pride. His transformation was slower than the team's. And in its own way, his acceptance was a milestone. Above him stood the big boss. When he had said, "Forget the DC cost," it wasn't an impulsive dismissal. It was a reminder that leaders must know which battles matter and which myths must be broken. He had an extraordinary ability to look past noise and study the signal. And then there was Mr. Sandeep, the logistics head. Sandeep gave us the mechanism to translate courage into movement. He didn't react dramatically when I emailed him about two rakes; he just replied with calm efficiency. That calmness was a form of leadership too. Together, this unlikely mix of cautious veterans, nervous managers, logical leaders, and practical executors created what I can only describe as a cultural chain reaction. No single person caused the domino effect; it was the collective chemistry of the group. One leader removed fear. One manager reluctantly accepted the change. One logistics head operationalized it. One team executed it. What began as a moment of madness was now a movement, a newly formed identity for the unit.

Those weeks were an unplanned leadership workshop for me. The first lesson was simple, almost embarrassingly simple: don't worship peanuts. For years, the entire dispatch culture had bowed before DC cost as though it were a deity. A tiny insignificant penalty compared to the larger operational landscape had occupied disproportionate space in their minds. I realized then how easily humans inflate small fears into giant obstacles. When you place a magnifying glass over a peanut, it looks like a boulder. And when enough people stare at that magnifying glass long enough, they begin believing the boulder is real. My job, I understood, was to gently remove the magnifying glass so they could see the peanut for what it was. The moment that illusion broke, half the battle was already won. The second lesson emerged from a single question: "Why only one rake?" Leadership, I learned, comes from asking the right questions. This is what is known the Challenger mind-set; the willingness to question assumptions so deeply ingrained that they've become invisible. My team wasn't lazy; they were conditioned. They weren't resistant; they were fearful. And fear survives best in silence. The moment a question breaks the silence, assumptions give way to logic. The third lesson was: courage is contagious. My team did not suddenly develop bravery; they borrowed it. They borrowed it from me in the early days, and I borrowed it from the big boss. Hence, courage might not always originate from within; sometimes it is transferred from one mind to another like a lit flame passed from one candle to the next. Eventually, every candle shines on its own, but someone has to light it first. The fourth lesson was accompanied by my forever friend, chaos. Moving from one rake to two, then three, then 3.5 was not a neat transition. It was messy and uncomfortable. Mistakes happened. Tempers flared. But amid that chaos, growth was also branching out. We associate progress with order, but real progress rarely looks orderly. It looks like confusion, it feels like uncertainty, and it sounds like disagreement. The fifth lesson revealed itself like a slow sunrise: fear shrinks as challenges expand. The day the team managed 3.5 rakes, I noticed no one celebrated dramatically. No one took selfies or posed next to wagons. Instead, they engaged in discussions about how to optimize further. The fear that once occupied their minds had evaporated, leaving behind a newly spacious mental landscape. And the moment that space became available, ambition rushed in to fill it. Human beings behave like silos: when fear fills the chamber, nothing else fits inside. But once fear is emptied out, innovation flows naturally. My team started suggesting improvements I hadn't even considered. Their confidence grew quietly.

When the dust finally settled over the months of experimentation, recalibration, and fearless dispatching, I often found myself standing near the sidings and watching the rakes move with a quiet sense of wonder. The transformation made me reflect on something deeper. It struck me that the entire journey wasn't truly about cement, dispatch, or logistics. It was about mind-set. It was a living illustration of a phenomenon motivational speakers sell, psychologists study, and management books romanticize: the shift from scarcity mind-set to abundance mind-set. Only here, it wasn't framed in fancy jargon or promoted through TED Talks. It happened in a dusty dispatch yard, among real people with real fears, real pressures, and real responsibilities. The fear of DC cost had kept the team chained to scarcity thinking. Every decision was rooted in avoidance. But once the team tasted the possibility of gain, their entire worldview changed. Their fears shrank. They stopped clutching the imaginary shield of safety and instead stepped into growth. And that, I realized, is the essence of leadership: multiplying courage. This psychological transition echoed in another subtle observation: the dispatch building had become emotionally lighter. There was more laughter during shift handovers. People narrated small victories with pride. Even failures didn't provoke panic anymore.

I remember one particular morning when I entered the dispatch office and overheard two supervisors debating whether a four-rake day was actually feasible. They weren't arguing to escape responsibility, they were arguing because both wanted to be the one who cracked the next milestone. That moment made me smile. If I had to summarise the entire rake revolution into one distilled insight, it would be this: growth begins where fear ends. And fear ends not when a leader eliminates risk, but when a leader makes the team feel safe enough to explore the risk together. In the larger picture of factory, the transition from one rake to 3.5 might seem like an operational milestone. But within the department, it felt like a cultural rebirth. The beauty of such transformations is that they rarely end where they begin. Long after the dispatch numbers stabilised, long after the excitement settled into routine, long after the dramatic days turned into memory, the mind-set stayed. And that is why the epilogue of this chapter writes itself: in manufacturing, in leadership, and in life, the world transforms not when the systems change, but when the beliefs do. And once a team learns to believe in itself, the story never ends. It only evolves.

Chapter 11
The Great Cement Civil War (PCC vs PPC)

Every industry has its silent wars at some point. Some are fought with pricing. Some with capacity. Ours was fought with colour. Grey versus not-quite-grey. Conventional certainty versus uncomfortable logic. Portland Pozzolana Cement (PPC) against Portland Composite Cement (PCC). It was one of the most emotionally charged internal battles I had witnessed in my career. At that time, our cement sales portfolio was simple and stable. PPC was king. Ninety percent of our volume came from it. Dealers trusted it and contractors demanded it. Engineers slept peacefully because PPC had decades of social approval behind it. It was familiar, predictable and most importantly safe. PCC, on the other hand, sat awkwardly at ten percent. It was technically sound, environmentally superior and economically sensible. But none of that mattered. Because PCC didn't *look* like cement was supposed to look.

The first serious conversation about increasing PCC share happened in a conference room. The whiteboard displayed the ratio 90:10. Everyone in the room knew what it meant. Changing that ratio wasn't a technical decision. It was a psychological one. The official reasons were noble. Reduced clinker factor. Lower carbon footprint. Conservation of limestone reserves. Sustainability goals that looked excellent in annual reports. Management wanted us to push PCC harder, to prepare for a future where resource efficiency would matter more than habit. Unofficially, everyone feared the same thing: market backlash. Dealers were the first line of resistance. Many of them had built their businesses on predictability. Grey cement meant trust. Grey meant strength. Grey meant "this is what my father sold and his father before him." PCC's lighter shade triggered immediate suspicion. To them, it looked diluted. Weak. Artificial. Contractors amplified that fear. They spoke in metaphors because metaphors felt safer than data. PCC looked like toothpaste. Like whitening powder. Like something that didn't belong in a column or slab. They worried about setting time, early strength, surface finish. They worried about explaining it to site supervisors who measured quality with instinct, not lab reports. Inside the company, the anxiety took another form. Sales teams feared complaints. Logistics feared returns. Finance feared inventory pile-ups. And management feared one thing above all: reputational damage from a product that might be right, but "felt" wrong.

I was sitting in the middle of this tension when something became clear to me. This wasn't a cement problem. This was a trust problem. People weren't rejecting PCC because it failed. They were rejecting it because they hadn't *seen* it succeed. So I decided to stop talking and start showing. The first battlefield was the construction site. The early demos were uncomfortable. Contractors stood with folded arms, watching the mix like referees waiting for a foul. Every comment was loaded. "Looks thin." "Doesn't feel heavy." "Is this really cement?" I learned quickly that countering fear with lectures didn't work. Charts made people defensive. What worked was patience and familiarity. We cast cubes. We waited. We tested. We didn't rush conclusions. Internally, the pressure was intense. Every failed demo would have reinforced every fear. I knew that. Management knew that. But there was no shortcut. PCC didn't win hearts in seven days. It needed time. Like many things that age better than they appear at first glance.

While sites tested strength, dealers tested courage. Stocking PCC meant risking shelf space on a product customers might question. It meant answering awkward questions. It meant being the first to say, "Try this." Convincing them required a different conversation. About where their business would stand five years later and whether safety lay in repeating the past or adapting before the market forced them to.

The first contractors who used PCC out of curiosity began noticing things they hadn't expected. Workability improved. Long-term strength matched, sometimes exceeded, PPC. Surface finish was cleaner. Once confidence entered their system, fear began to leak out. That's how I knew PCC had crossed its first invisible threshold. But before that happened, the pushback intensified. Internally, the biggest friction came from people who were neither against PCC nor fully for it.

They were cautious. They wanted proof, but not at their own expense. Every complaint from the field travelled faster than every success story. A delayed set, a colour mismatch, a confused mason. The irony was brutal. PPC had produced similar issues for decades, but familiarity made those problems invisible. PCC, being new, was guilty until proven innocent every single day.

Management reviews were becoming tense. I realized then that PCC's biggest challenge wasn't technical acceptance. It was organizational patience. Sales teams felt exposed. They were the ones facing contractors daily. They feared losing relationships built over years because of one forced push. So instead of pushing harder, we slowed down. We stopped positioning PCC as a replacement. We positioned it as a choice. Site demonstrations became more deliberate. We didn't cherry-pick results. We showed early strength honestly, even when PPC performed better at seven days. Then we stayed long enough for the 28-day results to speak for themselves. The credibility this built mattered more than any brochure.

One afternoon, during a lab visit, I watched a contractor stare silently at the compression testing machine. The PCC cube had just crossed the expected strength comfortably. He just nodded once, slowly. His nod meant more than any testimonial to me. From that point on, few contractors began recommending PCC to each other. "It's cheaper." "It gains strength with age." "Finish is better." They compared it to aging actors and long-term investments. PCC had stopped being our product. It had become their discovery.

Dealers felt the shift next. At first, they noticed it in small ways. Customers stopped asking why the cement looked different. They asked for it by name. Some even complained when PCC was unavailable. That's when stocking PCC stopped feeling like a risk and started feeling like a missed opportunity if not done. I remember a dealer calling me, his voice unusually animated. "Sir, earlier I was pushing PCC. Now customers are pushing me."

Inside the company, however, a new battle quietly emerged. It was the battle for credit. As PCC volumes began to rise, the resistance that had once been vocal changed tone. Earlier objections softened into reinterpretation. Conversations were rewritten retrospectively. What had once been called "too risky" was now described as "a bold but necessary experiment." What had once been dismissed as "market unreadiness" was reframed as "measured rollout." Fear was rebranded as foresight. People who had once warned passionately against PCC now spoke with calm authority about "phased adoption" and "balanced portfolios." Those who had demanded guarantees now spoke about "allowing the market to mature." It was fascinating to watch. Strategy decks quietly evolved. Slides were reordered. Timelines were adjusted so that scepticism appeared less absolute, hesitation less pronounced. In hindsight, everyone had been cautiously optimistic all along. Corporate memory, I learned, is not archival, it is adaptive. I didn't mind. By then, the objective had shifted. It was no longer about proving who was right or wrong. It was about making the transition irreversible.

The whiteboard ratios told the real story. They changed slowly, almost shyly, as if afraid to draw attention to themselves. Seventy-thirty. Then sixty-forty. This was the Blue Ocean we had stumbled into. At a certain point, it became clear that the shift from PPC to PCC represented more than a product transition. It marked a change in the competitive space itself. For years, PPC operated in a crowded, mature market. Every manufacturer sold it. Every dealer stocked it. Every contractor understood it. Competition focused on marginal gains and defensive positioning. PPC delivered reliability, yet it carried no distinct narrative. It functioned as a necessity rather than a differentiator. PCC entered the market on different terms. Instead of competing within existing expectations, it introduced a new basis of value. The focus moved toward long-term strength development, resource efficiency and sustainability. Discussions expanded beyond habit and familiarity toward outcome and lifecycle performance. Dealers gained a fresh story to share. Contractors gained a recommendation that reflected judgment rather than routine. This shift altered the dynamics of competition. While PPC remained locked in price-driven comparisons, PCC created a separate value space. It attracted attention through logic rather than promotion. In this new space, competitive pressure softened. Customers evaluated PCC on results rather than rivalry. The absence of direct comparison allowed the product to establish credibility on its own terms. Over time, imitation replaced scepticism and acceptance followed naturally. This was the essence of a blue ocean. The blue ocean emerged through persistence rather than disruption. There were no dramatic launches or aggressive mandates. Progress unfolded steadily through field results, consistent messaging and visible performance. The unfamiliar gradually became familiar. Confidence replaced caution. As volumes increased, PCC shifted from alternative to default. PPC continued to exist, yet the emotional centre of gravity moved. Conversations changed. Decisions accelerated. The organization adjusted its mind-set from defending tradition to shaping relevance.

In the next meeting, I walked into the same conference room where the debate had first begun. The room felt familiar, yet altered in a way that resisted immediate definition. The whiteboard stood at the front, freshly cleaned. Two numbers had been written in steady, unhurried handwriting:

- PCC - 90%
- PPC - 10%

I stood there longer than required, letting the meaning settle. The pause came from memory rather than surprise. I remembered the early days when even mentioning a fifty–fifty split triggered anxious debates. I remembered the long meetings, the raised eyebrows, the warnings framed as caution. I remembered how distant this ratio once felt, as theoretical as a future forecast that belonged to someone else's tenure. Now it sat there quietly, without justification. The Big Boss was already seated, tea in hand, his posture relaxed. He observed the room with the same patience that had defined his leadership throughout the transition. He listened as updates flowed around him, intervening only when clarity demanded it. Silence, in his presence, carried weight rather than discomfort. When someone eventually pointed toward the board and said, "We've crossed over," the room settled into a brief applause. The Big Boss followed the gesture, studied the numbers and nodded slowly, as if acknowledging a natural progression rather than a milestone. His expression carried calm assurance rather than triumph. "Well done," he said. "Cement is not just grey anymore." Across the table, the Boss exhaled deeply, the tension of months finally leaving his shoulders. The same man who once measured risk in sleepless nights allowed himself a half-smile. "I always knew PCC would win," he said, more to the room than to anyone in particular. I remained silent. I knew he didn't.

By now, PCC had moved beyond its identity as a product. It behaved like a default. Dealers placed orders without hesitation. Contractors specified it in BOQs without accompanying explanations. Sales teams stopped juggling parallel narratives and focused on execution. Even logistics adapted seamlessly, dispatching white bags with the same indifference once reserved for grey. The transition no longer demanded attention. It had embedded itself into routine. As the meeting shifted toward operational matters and future planning, the whiteboard remained untouched. The numbers stayed where they were, complete and self-sufficient. Walking out of the room, I understood that this moment marked more than a successful transition. It reflected the quiet strength of consistency, patience and trust in process. The war had ended without ceremony, because the outcome had already settled in the minds that mattered most. PCC succeeded because it reshaped what customers valued, rather than competing harder on existing dimensions. This experience reinforced a lasting principle: strategy gains power when it creates space rather than conflict. The most enduring advantages arise from redefining value and allowing the market to follow evidence over time.

Looking back, the PCC transition taught me more about leadership than any formal role ever did. First, I learned that data alone doesn't persuade. People don't argue with numbers; they argue with what numbers threaten. PCC threatened familiarity. The moment we understood that, our strategy changed. We stopped fighting logic battles and started building emotional safety. Second, I learned that resistance is a signal, not an obstacle. Every objection pointed to a fear; fear of loss, embarrassment, accountability. Address the fear and the resistance dissolves on its own. Third, I learned that credibility compounds. The first demo barely moved the needle. The tenth created curiosity. The fortieth created belief. Change isn't linear; it's cumulative. Each small success stacked quietly until disbelief became irrational. Fourth, I learned that leadership is about absorption. Absorbing anxiety from above. Absorbing frustration from below. Absorbing uncertainty long enough so others don't have to carry it all at once. The leader doesn't push change forward; the leader stands still while the organization leans forward at its own pace. And finally, I learned that blue oceans aren't discovered, they're constructed. One site at a time. One dealer conversation at a time. One uncomfortable meeting at a time. Strategy textbooks describe blue oceans like maps. In reality, they are built drop by drop, under scepticism and quiet doubt.

Long after PCC became dominant, I would still hear jokes. Someone would point at a white bag and say, "Sir, toothpaste cement." We'd laugh. One evening, much later, I found myself alone in that same conference room. The whiteboard was blank again, waiting for the next battle. I stood there for a moment, marker in hand, realizing something subtle but profound. This chapter of my career wasn't about cement at all. It was about how organizations learn through lived proof. Through watching someone stand by an idea long after it stops being fashionable to doubt it. PCC had taught us to tolerate discomfort, delay validation and trust process over panic. As I walked out, I glanced back once more at the board. I imagined the old ratio, the arguments, the anxiety. Then I erased it in my mind. Because the next civil war would come soon enough. It always does. And when it does, I know exactly how it will start; with something that looks different, feels risky and quietly asks the same dangerous question: Why not?

Chapter 12
The Interview Circus

"Hiring is like running a kiln — if you don't control the heat, you either burn the product or underfire the batch."

I did not invent that line at the time. I understood it only much later.

When I received the nomination for a program titled Evaluate for Hiring Engineers and Managers, my expectations remained modest. Experience had taught me that most HR trainings followed a familiar pattern: colourful slides, polite participation and Powerpoint fatigue. I entered the program prepared to endure it. But it turned out to be a full-blown masterclass on human psychology wrapped in corporate grammar. The trainer was an old HR wizard. He carried a permanent half-smile, the expression of a man who had listened patiently to decades of confident nonsense and survived.

He began without ceremony. "Why do we take feedback before an interview?" he asked. The room offered safe answers. Alignment. Context. Preparedness. I raised my hand. "To start judging before the person enters the room?" He laughed. "Exactly," he said. "Feedback is only useful if you don't let it bias you.

Judge potential, not performance. And please, stop asking yes-or-no questions. You're not interrogating terrorists."

Until then, I had believed interviews were about confirmation. Confirming competence. Confirming experience. Confirming fit. The training forced me to confront an uncomfortable truth: most interviews merely rewarded confidence and punished reflection. We hired the best talkers and then wondered why the best workers felt invisible. From that day, I made a quiet decision. I would listen less to what candidates said and more to how they thought. I would seek patterns. Stories, not statements.

The interview circus began soon after.

Interview #1: The Sentence Maintainer

My first real test arrived on a Teams call with a senior engineer. The fan behind him spun with impressive enthusiasm, compensating generously for the speed of his thoughts.

"Please introduce yourself," I said.

He began confidently. Too confidently.

"Myself Ramesh Kumar, working as senior engineer, having good exposure to preventive maintenance, predictive maintenance, shutdown maintenance, breakdown maintenance—"

I interrupted gently. "You also do maintenance of the sentence?"

He froze. For a brief moment, panic flickered across his face. Then he laughed nervously.

"Yes sir," he said, "all types of maintenance."

That honesty earned him more credit than his introduction ever could.

Later, I asked him what the last book he read was.

"Sir," he replied proudly, "manual of coal mill."

It was the most authentic answer of the day. He had not read a management bestseller. He had read the document that saved his bearing. In a world obsessed with appearing well-read, this man had quietly stayed useful.

Interview #2: The MBA Monk

The next candidate joined like a management poster child. MBA. Six Sigma Black Belt. Lean. Kaizen. TPM. 5S. I half-expected ABS and ESP to appear next.

"Sir," he began, "I am a certified Black Belt."

"Good," I replied. "You will need martial arts skills when the kiln trips at 2 AM."

He laughed. Always a promising sign.

When I asked how he managed work-life balance, he responded like a movie trailer.

"By accepting challenges, fighting them, resolving them and moving ahead."

I nodded. "Sounds like a motivational YouTube reel."

He smiled, unfazed. Then added, “The key lies in taking control of the plant before the plant controls you.”

That line was gold. Later, we used it in a safety campaign. He joined the organization soon after. Degrees had opened the door. Habits had sealed the decision.

Interview #3: The Discipline Distributor

The next candidate applied for Head - Operations & Maintenance. His tie had seen more shutdowns than most engineers.

“Sir,” he said confidently, “I have led three hundred people during shutdowns.”

“Did they follow you voluntarily,” I asked, “or because you blocked the exit?”

The panel laughed.

“I believe in strict discipline,” he continued. “Everyone must report by eight AM.”

“And you?” I asked.

“I usually reach by nine.”

At least he was honest.

When asked how he developed his team, he replied, “Sir, I send them for training… if budget permits.”

“And if budget does not permit?”

He grinned. “Then I send them mentally.”

That man was born for middle management; motivational in meetings, missing in action later.

Interview #4: The Single-Handed Saviour

Another candidate leaned forward and declared, "Sir, I single-handedly solved major breakdowns."

"Single-handedly?" I asked. "So others were clapping?"

"No sir," he replied seriously. "They were learning."

"Excellent," I said. "Next time, charge tuition fees."

He described how he reduced vibration by changing a bearing.

"Excellent!," I said. "Try reducing vibration next time by changing the engineer."

He smiled, unsure whether to laugh or revise his résumé.

By the time the fourth interview ended, I stopped thinking of interviews as conversations. They felt closer to stress tests. People fail quietly. The challenge lies in spotting the quiet failures early. The next candidate taught me that lesson without speaking much at all.

Interview #5: The Silent Saint

He joined the call precisely on time. The background looked minimalist, intentional, almost monk-like. He nodded respectfully and waited.

"Tell me something about yourself," I said.

He smiled. Peacefully. Said nothing. I waited. He waited better. I repeated the question, slightly slower.

"Sir," he said calmly, "everything is written in my CV."

"That is helpful," I replied, "but I lack telepathic abilities."

He smiled again. "Sir, I believe actions speak louder than words."

"True," I said, "interviews still require words."

Silence returned.

The panel shifted in their seats. Even the Teams camera seemed unsure whether to stay awake. That interview ended without conflict, drama or clarity. The candidate had confidence, composure and zero communication instinct. On the shop floor, silence can signal focus. In leadership, it often signals avoidance.

As interviews accumulated, patterns emerged with uncomfortable clarity. Candidates spoke fluently about systems yet struggled to describe a single failure. They listed achievements confidently and delegated responsibility retroactively. Many had managed large teams on paper while remaining strangely absent from any story involving people. Whenever I asked, "Tell me about a mistake," the answers followed familiar routes:

- "Sir, I work too hard."
- "Sir, I trust people too much."
- "Sir, I get emotionally involved."

Each response avoided discomfort while sounding virtuous. Experience had taught them how to dodge vulnerability with style. Then came the outliers. Those who paused, asked for a moment and admitted confusion, fear or misjudgement. They rarely sounded impressive. But they sounded real.

Interview #6: The GM of Wit

The final interview of the day carried a different energy. Interview for General Manager (O&M). The candidate joined with the calm of someone who had seen kilns trip, fans burst, belts tear and still smiled for group photographs afterward.

"What is the difference between a manager and a leader?" I asked.

"A manager does what is told," he said. "A leader does what is required."

The room leaned forward.

When asked about his biggest failure, he replied without hesitation, "Once, I believed management would appreciate honesty."

The panel dissolved into laughter.

He continued, "I learned that timing matters as much as truth."

Then he narrated a story.

He added, "Sir, I once convinced our MD not to delay a shutdown by comparing it to stopping a wedding because the band was late."

He paused.

"You cannot delay the wedding," he said. "You change the band."

The analogy landed perfectly.

We hired him instantly. The man was pure gold, part engineer, part stand-up comedian, full leader.

Manufacturing teaches lessons that management books avoid: confidence collapses at 2 AM, titles disappear during breakdowns. On the shop floor, humility survives. Ego fails quickly. The interviews that day confirmed something I had begun to suspect: education equips knowledge, experience sharpens skill, but self-awareness determines longevity. Candidates who laughed at themselves survived stress better. Those who took themselves seriously cracked faster. Humour acted as a pressure valve. It released tension, revealed adaptability and exposed insecurity when absent. Anyone who could smile after being challenged possessed resilience. Anyone who felt offended carried fragility disguised as authority.

After enough interviews, a strange reversal takes place. You stop evaluating candidates. You start evaluating the panel. The questions remain the same, the faces change, but the reactions inside the room become predictable. Someone always leans toward familiarity. Someone gravitates toward confidence. Someone equates silence with depth and fluency with intelligence. The interview begins revealing less about the candidate and more about the biases seated around the table. I started noticing it in the pauses. Whenever a candidate spoke fluent English with corporate rhythm, heads nodded instinctively. Whenever someone struggled to articulate thoughts, pens paused. The content mattered less than the packaging. Years of conditioning surfaced quietly. The panel believed it was objective. It rarely was.

One candidate arrived with average credentials and extraordinary articulation. He spoke in structured paragraphs, answered crisply and maintained eye contact with textbook precision. Every response sounded interview-ready. The panel loved him. Then I asked a simple question. "Describe a situation where your decision made the problem worse." He smiled confidently. Then spoke for three minutes without answering it. I repeated the question. He reframed it. I pushed again. Eventually, the structure collapsed. The confidence thinned. What remained was surface-level experience wrapped in practiced delivery. That interview reinforced a hard truth: communication skills may amplify thinking but cannot replace it.

Another candidate joined with hesitant English and strong technical grounding. His sentences arrived slowly. Grammar stumbled. Ideas took time. The panel grew restless. I interrupted gently and said, "Take your time. I am listening." He relaxed visibly. Once the pressure eased, he spoke with more clarity. His understanding of systems, failure modes and maintenance philosophy surpassed many fluent speakers earlier that day. He spoke in fewer words, yet each word carried weight. The panel noticed, slightly embarrassed. That candidate received unanimous approval by the end.

By then, humour had become deliberate. I used it carefully to observe the behaviour of the candidate. A light joke early in the interview acted like a stress test. Candidates who smiled and responded demonstrated adaptability. Those who froze revealed rigidity. Those who felt offended displayed insecurity. One candidate laughed at himself after a playful challenge and said, "Sir, I deserved that." Another stiffened and corrected my phrasing. Both reactions told complete stories. Manufacturing environments reward those who absorb shock without cracking. Humour measures that capacity faster than psychometric tests. Anyone who survives a kiln trip survives a joke.

The panel often chased a dangerous illusion: perfect fit. "Culture fit" became shorthand for comfort. Candidates who resembled existing leaders felt safe. Those who challenged norms felt risky. I began pushing back with my philosophy that a perfect fit can stagnate organizations while useful friction can strengthen them. I asked candidates questions to create mild discomfort such as "What company policy would you challenge?" or "Tell me something you disagree with in our industry." Or "Describe a time you pushed back against authority." Safe candidates answered cautiously. Valuable candidates answered thoughtfully. Disagreement, when respectful, signals engagement. Compliance signals survival instinct.

One interview involved a candidate with decades of experience and a résumé thick enough to require binding. Every answer began with, "In my thirty years…" Experience had given him authority. It had also hardened his thinking. When asked about adapting to new technology, he replied, "New systems create more problems than solutions." When asked about younger engineers, he said, "They lack commitment." When asked about learning, he said, "At this stage, I guide rather than learn." The panel hesitated. We passed.

Hiring always involves risk. Avoiding risk produces mediocrity. Managing risk produces growth. I stopped seeking certainty and sought indicators such as learning velocity, self-awareness, resilience under pressure. These indicators outperformed experience metrics repeatedly. The interview circus taught me that organizations rarely suffer from lack of talent. By the end of that phase, a rule formed quietly in my mind: hire people who make the panel slightly uncomfortable, yet intellectually curious.

Chapter 13
The Performance Appraisal Meltdown

"In performance appraisals, truth passes through the same process as cement — mixed, molded and compressed into something completely different."

The day finally arrived. Performance Appraisal Day. My manager called me into his cabin with the solemnity of a man about to announce either a promotion or a policy change.

"Let's discuss your performance," he said.

I straightened my collar, picked up my diary, thicker than most OEM manuals and walked in with the confidence of a freshly lubricated bearing ready for inspection. His cabin looked unchanged. He gestured for me to sit.

He began gently. "So," he asked, leaning back, "how's your family?"

I smiled politely. This question never appeared in the KPI framework, but experience had taught me that appraisals often began with emotional warm-up before analytical ambush.

"Everyone is well, sir," I replied.

He nodded, satisfied, as if domestic stability directly correlated with equipment uptime. Then came the swerve.

"So," he said casually, "what did you do this year?"

That question deserved a pause. Instead, I responded instinctively, like a system dump triggered under pressure. I delivered my year in bullet points, crisp and efficient:

- Early stabilization and commissioning.
- Highest production figures in plant history.
- Lowest monthly power consumption achieved.
- Early PG clearance of OEM equipment.
- Safety systems implemented with zero lost-time incidents.
- Team training across technical and safety domains.
- Budget adherence and inventory discipline.

Each line landed tick mark in my opinion. He nodded through every point, slowly, rhythmically, like a meditation instructor guiding a breathing exercise. Then he leaned back, folded his hands and asked the question that has haunted professionals across industries and decades.

"Tell me something unique."

Unique? The word echoed in my head like a plant alarm. Unique compared to what? I scanned my mental inventory. What was left? Catching the moon with a torque wrench?

I asked carefully, "Sir, could you please elaborate?"

He smiled. That calm, managerial smile reserved for moments where clarification would dilute authority.

"No," he said. "This is your time. What you never told me before. How can I rate you now?"

That was when my internal kiln tripped. The realization hit hard: my entire year, shutdowns, breakdowns, early mornings, late nights, safety drills, cost controls, had already passed through the appraisal mixer. Now it awaited compression.

I muttered, "Sir, I tried my best."

He nodded once. "Good."

And just like that, twelve months of effort, responsibility and stress compressed into a three-minute nods. The meeting ended politely. I walked out intact, yet slightly reduced in volume, like clinker that had cooled too fast.

The following week, HR released the sacred chart. The Bell Curve. Every engineer's fate plotted like a temperature graph.

5 Outstanding

4 Exceeds Expectations

3 Meets Expectations

2 Needs Improvement

1 Below Expectations

The shop floor translations, however, told a different story.

- Outstanding usually meant either preventing a catastrophe or having a manager who needed a favour returned.
- Exceeds Expectations implied solid work combined with superior storytelling.
- Meets Expectations meant you survived, attendance achieved, meetings endured.
- Needs Improvement often followed honesty in self-review.
- Below Expectations sometimes traced its origins to a single disagreement in a morning meeting.

No matter how many shutdowns were saved or how many nights were sacrificed, the curve demanded symmetry. The same organization that preached teamwork now required ranking teammates against each other. People who had solved problems together sat side by side, silently assigned to different categories, pretending nothing had changed.

Soon enough, the curve turned its gaze toward me. It was my turn to rate others. I opened Excel, the modern courtroom of corporate justice. Three names stared back at me: Bharat, Sandeep and Prakash. Each represented a different philosophy of work. Each carried strengths, flaws and unintended comedy. The irony struck me immediately. A week ago, I had felt compressed. Now I held the compressor. And that realization came with weight. Because appraisals reveal character less through ratings and more through intent. They expose whether leaders rate for compliance, comfort or growth.

Case 1: Bharat - The Breakdown Buddha

Bharat belonged to Mechanical Maintenance. His defining quality was availability. If something moved, stopped moving or looked like it might consider stopping, Bharat appeared.

"Sir," he said proudly during his appraisal discussion, "twenty-nine breakdowns handled this year."

I looked at him. "And how many did you prevent?"

He paused, thought seriously and replied, "None, sir. But all were closed quickly."

That sentence summarized his philosophy. Bharat thrived on action. He reacted faster than alarms. He treated breakdowns like opportunities rather than failures. Once, during a routine inspection, he pressed an emergency stop unintentionally and reported, with complete sincerity, "Sir, system testing successful." His optimism could start a generator. Predictive maintenance, in his world, happened immediately after failure. Preventive maintenance existed mostly as an intention. Still, when equipment failed at inconvenient hours, Bharat answered the phone. I stared at the rating options. Giving him a high rating rewarded fire-fighting. Giving him a low rating punished availability. The system offered no space for nuance. I chose the middle.

Three out of five. The comment box demanded diplomacy. I typed: "Always ready for action - mostly his own." The cursor blinked, satisfied.

Case 2: Sandeep - The Spreadsheet Samurai

Sandeep worked in Process. His strength lay in data. He arrived at his appraisal with charts prepared, trends highlighted and a backup pendrive in case destiny attacked the primary one.

"Sir," he announced confidently, "zero breakdowns in my area."

I nodded. Then asked, "Then what about these three kiln stoppages?"

He smiled calmly. "Power failure, sir. Not my scope."

Sandeep owned uptime with pride and outsourced downtime with elegance. His power-saving innovation involved adjusting a knob slightly and documenting it extensively. Still, his reports made sense. His analysis prevented several inefficiencies before they escalated. He delivered clarity. He lacked ownership during discomfort. The rating scale stared back at me again. Four felt generous. Three felt unfair. The half-star option tempted compromise. I chose three-point-five. The comment read: "Analytical strength with strong reporting; accountability software pending update." Excel accepted it without emotion.

Case 3: Prakash - The Innovator of Missing Jigs

Prakash belonged to Projects and Utilities. Energy followed him. So did chaos.

"Sir," he said enthusiastically, "I designed a new alignment jig. Saved one hour of maintenance time."

I asked, "Documented?"

"No sir," he replied cheerfully. "Told night shift orally."

The next morning, the jig disappeared. By the weekend, four variations existed. One served as a door stopper near the MCC room. Prakash solved one problem by creating two. His creativity flowed faster than he could control. He improved processes, then forgot to institutionalize them. Yet, his intent leaned forward. His mistakes came from speed, not negligence. Four out of five. The comment read: "Creative and proactive; requires innovation with instruction manual."

Bonus Case - The Ghost Performer

Then came the surprise. A name appeared that triggered mild confusion. The individual had resigned six months earlier. The system remembered him faithfully. Rating required. Meets Expectations. After all, he met expectations perfectly by leaving and never returning. I closed that row with quiet irony.

I leaned back and stared at the spreadsheet. This document would travel upward, stripped of context, reduced to averages and colours. Names would blur. Scores would remain. The bell curve would smile politely. I saved the file. One truth settled firmly:

appraisal systems claim to measure performance, yet they reveal character primarily of the person doing the rating.

Thereafter, the calibration meeting happened like a courtroom session without witnesses. Managers defended their ratings nervously. HR nodded thoughtfully. Senior leadership leaned back, hands folded, projecting neutrality. "This team has too many fours," someone said. I replied, "This year demanded too much." Silence followed. Context felt unwelcome. The curve preferred clean shapes to messy explanations. One senior voice intervened. "We must maintain differentiation." Differentiation from what? I thought. The discussion shifted from performance to optics. How would this distribution look across departments? Would compensation budgets stretch? People became mere data points. I watched capable engineers slide from fours to threes without discussion. Their work remained unchanged. Only their representation shifted.

What disturbed me most came later, during feedback conversations. Appraisal language mastered the art of sounding kind while delivering reduction.

"You have met expectations." Translation: You did enough to avoid attention.

"There is scope for improvement." Translation: You made someone uncomfortable.

"You should be more visible." Translation: Your work failed to travel upward.

"We value your contribution." Translation: Please accept this number quietly.

People nodded politely while internal equations recalculated futures. Promotions delayed. Confidence dented. Motivation quietly taxed. Appraisals claimed to encourage growth. They often produced compliance instead.

One engineer sat across from me during feedback, posture stiff, notebook open.

"Sir," he said carefully, "what should I improve?"

I paused.

I answered honestly. "Your work speaks clearly. Your presence remains quiet."

He nodded. "So I should talk more?"

"Yes," I said. "And write."

It bothered me to answer in such a blunt way. Since when did articulation outrank execution! I remember my early appraisal cycles clearly. I was not articulate but I was effective. I did not know how to convert twelve-hour shifts into tidy sentences. I did not know how to turn a prevented failure into a bullet point. When appraisal time came, I walked in carrying notebooks stained with grease. And initially I struggled, like the young engineers struggling now. When asked, "What did you achieve this year?" my mind would stall. Not because there was nothing to say, but because the nature of my work resisted storytelling. How do you describe something that did not fail? How do you prove a disaster that never occurred? Meanwhile, others spoke fluently. They spoke about initiatives, ownership, improvements and alignment. Their language filled the room even when their contribution barely reached the shop floor. They sounded so impressive. I was rated two out of five.

I have come to accept the appraisal system even though I never agreed with it. Here is the truth most leaders avoid: Appraisal damage does not come from low ratings.

It comes from unexplained ratings. A two with clarity gives direction. A three without explanation creates a false sense of relief. I know this because I lived it. I accepted shortcomings easily. I could handle correction. What I could not handle was invisibility, the feeling that effort had passed through the organization unnoticed, reduced to a number that explained nothing. Years later, whenever I sit on the other side of the table, that memory returns with force. Two engineers could receive the same rating while carrying vastly different burdens. One solved visible problems, the other prevented invisible disasters. The system rewarded the first. This is where appraisal logic fails manufacturing reality. In manufacturing, success often appears as absence. Absence of accidents and breakdowns. Appraisal systems struggle with absence. They thrive on presence as it is easier to record. But the best-performing plants rarely look dramatic. They look mundane and predictable.

Looking back, I think I understand why articulation overtook execution. Organizations rely on summaries, narratives and indicators. The ability to translate work gradually becomes as valuable as the work itself. That is understandable. What is not acceptable is forgetting the cost. When presentation eclipses persistence, cultures tend to drift. People stop investing in prevention because prevention rarely gets applause. They wait for visible problems because visible problems generate recognition. That is how accidents are sometimes born from incentive structures that reward reaction over discipline. As a young engineer, I felt this pressure without being able to name it. I stayed late fixing problems quietly and wondered why my ratings always felt lighter than my effort.

By the time I oversaw appraisals myself, one truth had hardened beyond debate. That Performance appraisals reveal less about performance and more about organizational courage. Where that courage is absent organisational cultures degrade quietly. I saw it in younger engineers who reminded me of myself, who were capable, diligent, but uncomfortable in appraisal rooms. I recognized the hesitation, the silence, the forced acceptance of numbers that explained barely explained anything.

Chapter 14
The Great Housekeeping Abhiyaan

Every cement plant celebrates few festivals that do not appear on the official calendar. One of them is the housekeeping drive. It begins with a well-worded email carrying moral authority far beyond its font size. The subject line always sounds harmless "Cleanliness is next to godliness," yet everyone knows what follows. This time, the message came with greater gravity.

Day 1: The Awakening

By 9:30 AM, the General Manager called a meeting. His voice was calm, which made the message more dangerous.

"The super-boss will visit soon," he said. "The plant must look like a bride."

Silence followed. Somewhere at the back, someone whispered, "Sir, currently she looks like her grandmother."

Laughter tried to escape, failed and disguised itself as throat-clearing.

Operation Abhiyaan had begun.

The kickoff meeting felt louder than the preheater fan, even though no one raised their voice. Posters appeared overnight, planted strategically by HR like motivational landmines.

Swachhata Abhiyaan. Clean Plant, Green Planet. Clean Today, Safe Tomorrow.

One technician, clearly overwhelmed by inspiration, added his own handwritten slogan near the pump house: Clean before boss arrives or you'll be cleaned from payroll.

HR pretended not to notice. Everyone else took photos.

Departments exchanged glances that carried silent questions: Who will clean what? Who decides what is scrap and what is heritage? So we began with a plant walk-through. This is where denial collapses. The preheater floors looked like a desert ecosystem. Layers of dust had settled with geological commitment. Each layer represented a phase of plant history. The cooler deck wore a permanent grey carpet. Even the floor markings had surrendered. The kiln walkway resembled a museum, artifacts everywhere, explanations nowhere. Someone kicked the floor gently. Dust responded enthusiastically.

"Sir," my supervisor asked cautiously, "do we get extra manpower?"

"Yes," I said solemnly. "Each man will get the power of two."

Brooms emerged hesitantly. This is always the most awkward phase. Engineers do not sweep instinctively. They analyse the broom first. Someone asked whether sweeping fell under mechanical, civil or safety scope. Another checked if gloves were mandatory. The first sweep raised a dust cloud. Visibility dropped instantly. People disappeared into grey fog like explorers testing a hostile planet. Someone coughed dramatically. Someone else blamed allergies. The dust remained unimpressed. By noon, nothing looked cleaner. Everything looked worse.

Day 1: Resistance never looks like protest.

It looks like slow movement, frequent discussions and urgent phone calls that suddenly appear. One engineer spent thirty minutes debating whether a pile of scrap qualified as "usable later." Another searched for approval to move a rusted trolley that had not moved since commissioning. Housekeeping forces confrontation with neglected decisions. Lunch broke the tension slightly. Post-lunch, people returned with a new energy and stopped asking who should clean. They started cleaning what annoyed them most. Ownership was emerging quietly. By evening, it became clear why Day 1 always feels the hardest. Housekeeping forces visibility. It exposes disorder we learn to ignore. It challenges the comfort of familiarity. It removes excuses. By sunset, the plant looked marginally better and emotionally exhausted. Dust still dominated. Progress remained uneven. Next day, the makeover would begin.

Day 2: The Marriage Makeover

If Day 1 was acceptance, Day 2 was action with consequences. Tractor-trolleys rolled in before the morning tea finished brewing, lining up at the gate like a wedding baraat. The only music was honking. Helpers jumped down with brooms held like rifles. Welders arrived carrying paintbrushes. Fitters debated loudly about whether sweeping counted as mechanical scope or civil intrusion. Electricians offered moral support and extension cords. The gardener showed up, smiling, convinced this was some version of Van Mahotsav. The makeover had begun.

The preheater floors resisted first. Years of accumulation had bonded it to steel and concrete with emotional attachment. The first sweep raised clouds thick enough to reset everyone's sense of direction. Two technicians with air-blowers stepped in and vanished instantly. For a full minute, only the sound of motors confirmed their existence. When they reappeared, helmets, faces, jackets, everything shared the same shade of grey. They looked like astronauts returning from Mars, disappointed by the lack of oxygen and surprised by the gravity. Communication turned into hand signals.

One supervisor walked confidently into a pillar he had passed daily for three years.

By mid-morning, plans surrendered to improvisation. Brooms ran out. Someone discovered that discarded conveyor belt pieces worked surprisingly well as scrapers. Compressed air hoses became multi-purpose weapons, capable of cleaning floors and starting political debates when misdirected. A team used wooden planks to drag dust into manageable piles, calling it "bulk handling optimization." One helper tried wiping his face with a dirty rag and became half-painted like Lord Hanuman. I told him, "Don't move — we'll make you the mascot of commitment."

The most remarkable change happened. Nobody asked who was responsible anymore. People cleaned what annoyed them. Corners that had irritated eyes for years suddenly became targets. A junior engineer repainted a railing without asking. A supervisor reorganized a cable tray area he had avoided for months. Security polished the gate signage until the numbers reflected faces clearly.

By late afternoon, fatigue set in. Shirts stiffened with dust. Helmets bore permanent grey tattoos. Backs complained quietly. Yet faces glowed with a different light. Progress had become visible. Cleaned sections stood out sharply against untouched areas. Contrast motivated faster than any instruction. Teams began competing silently. One group cleaned stairs nobody used. Another polished handrails near the administrative block. Someone cleaned behind an MCC panel and discovered artifacts from commissioning days, bolts, washers and a forgotten coffee cup with a logo that had rebranded twice. History revealed itself layer by layer.

Movement changed thinking. Once bodies engaged, minds followed. Stress dissipated through action. Complaints reduced as effort increased. Physical work simplified emotional complexity. One engineer said, "Earlier I was stressed about breakdowns. Today I am too tired to worry." That sentence explained the day.

Day 3: Road to Glory

Day 3 was about surfaces that could be photographed. The first agenda item was roads and walkways. Roads in cement plants age faster than employees. They absorb weight, spills, shortcuts and indifference. Over time, markings fade, edges crumble and everyone adjusts mentally. Day 3 demanded reversal of that adjustment. Paint drums appeared early. Brushes multiplied mysteriously. A team debated whether zebra crossings should follow traffic rules or artistic freedom. Someone suggested measuring spacing. Someone else suggested eyeballing it. Eyeballing won. The first crossing looked confident. The second looked enthusiastic. By the third, stripes spread like butter on hot paratha. Walkways followed next. Handrails were repainted with optimism and varying interpretations of "straight." Some rails shone brilliantly. Others displayed artistic curves suggesting wind resistance studies. Safety inspected quietly and chose peace. Yellow lines appeared on floors marking walk zones. For the first time, people walked where lines suggested rather than where habit dictated. That alone justified the effort. Directional signboards were done mid-morning. Someone discovered old boards stored behind the warehouse. They were dusted, repainted and reinstalled with pride. Two arrows pointed in opposite directions, both reading “Packing Plant →.” Confusion was now well-organised.

Day 4: The KPI Carnival

The super-boss was due soon. So Day 4 belonged to KPIs. By morning, the plant began transforming again theatrically. Departments erected KPI displays big enough to stop a dumper. Flex banners stretched proudly and charts bloomed like seasonal flowers. Maintenance went first, as always. Their board stood tall, bold letters screaming ZERO BREAKDOWN in triumphant font. The chart was clean, symmetrical and printed on expensive paper. Five minutes later, a forklift broke down right behind the board. “Relax,” I said. “It’s a live demonstration.”

Electrical decided that numbers needed ambience. They added fairy lights around their KPI chart. The board glowed like a wedding mandap. Power factor values sparkled. Energy consumption curves shimmered.

By afternoon, the plant resembled a fairground. Charts competed for attention. Words like World-Class, Best-in-Class and Benchmark appeared without supporting witnesses. Engineers stood near their boards, rehearsing explanations like students before viva. Supervisors practiced pointing gestures. Managers memorized which KPI to mention first. Everyone knew the numbers mattered less than confidence in explaining them.

I walked through the plant slowly, watching engineers defend charts with genuine passion. People wanted to be seen as competent, responsible, in control. Every engineer knew the real heroes of the plant rarely appeared on KPI boards. The guy who prevented a failure quietly. The supervisor who stayed late solving a problem nobody documented. The fitter who fixed something permanently instead of temporarily. Their work lived between numbers. Day 4 reminded me why performance management feels exhausting.

Day 5: The GM with the Belcha

Day 5 brought something entirely different and symbolic. The General Manager walked into the yard earlier than usual. He stood still for a moment. Then he spotted a clinker heap near the transfer point. He walked toward it. Someone noticed and reacted instinctively. "Sir, that's clinker!" The GM picked up a belcha lying nearby and smiled. "Doesn't matter. It's still grey and in my way." The belcha moved. Clinker shifted. History was rewritten.

The effect was immediate and irreversible. People stopped watching and started moving. Helpers swept harder. Engineers bent lower. Supervisors put phones away. The crane operator climbed down and cleaned his cabin meticulously, possibly inspired, possibly terrified, likely both. No orders were given. The message travelled faster than any circular. Phones appeared, of course. Photos were taken and videos recorded. Someone joked about LinkedIn posts. The GM ignored it all, focusing on the heap in front of him.

Until Day 5, housekeeping felt like a mission to impress someone else. After the belcha moment, it became personal. People began correcting each other gently. Dirty corners were revisited voluntarily. Tools were returned to proper places without reminders. There was a change in the spoken words even.

Earlier:

"Sir, should we clean this also?" "Sir, is this required?"

After GM's belcha moment: "Let's finish this properly." "This area still looks off."

That's the power of leadership done right.

Day 6: From old lady to bride

The transformation was complete. Someone said it out loud, finally giving shape to what everyone was thinking. "Sir, earlier the plant looked like an old lady who gave up on makeup," he said, scanning the yard slowly. "Now she looks like a bride ready for a photoshoot." Someone said "We are artists." We all agreed.

That evening, the plant glowed. Lights reflected off clean surfaces. Roads guided trucks smoothly. Railings caught light just enough to feel intentional. Trucks rolled in slowly, almost respectfully, as if attending a reception rather than a dispatch bay. The bride metaphor no longer felt exaggerated. The cooler area once referred to unofficially as the grey zone, had undergone a quiet resurrection. Cleaned thoroughly, repainted carefully, lit properly. Someone took a selfie. Then another. Then a group photo. The idea that engineers would take photos inside a cement plant would have sounded absurd a week earlier.

People care deeply about their environment when they feel ownership. Cleanliness is not about mops or paint. It is about dignity. When disorder dominates, people shrink internally. When order returns, confidence follows. The plant did not just look better. It felt better. We knew the Abhiyaan was ending. That awareness brought a strange mix of relief and reluctance. The Great Housekeeping Abhiyaan had changed behaviour without enforcement.

Day 7: Inspection drama

The frantic energy of earlier days had dissolved. The plant stood ready for any inspection. The super-boss was due that morning. Everyone knew the routine. White helmet. Clean shoes. We gathered near the gate and waited. The convoy entered. The super-boss stepped out, immaculate, as if dust had never existed in his universe. He looked around slowly. He scanned the roads first, eyes tracing the zebra crossings that now actually resembled zebras rather than abstract art. We followed him like nervous interns, careful to stay close without obstructing his way. He walked the roads deliberately, observing how trucks moved, how pedestrians behaved, how lines were respected.

He tapped the preheater floor: no dust came off. “Excellent.” Then he spotted one trolley corner full of scrap.

“Why is that still here?”

I whispered, "Sir, emotional attachment since commissioning."

He laughed, "Remove emotions ASAP."

He paused at the KPI displays. He scanned them without lingering too long. It seemed like numbers interested him less. "Looks structured," he said. That dismantled half the anxiety built over four days. When the inspection ended, he exchanged few final words and shook some hands. The convoy left quietly. The plant exhaled. We had survived. When the photos finally went to corporate, we looked heroic.

The plant slowly returned to routine. Machines resumed their usual conversations. Trucks came and went. Dispatch schedules reclaimed authority. The General Manager called for a small ceremony. Certificates were handed out, titled "Champions of Cleanliness". Then he unveiled the belcha. The same belcha he had picked up days earlier now sat mounted in a simple frame. He looked at us and said quietly, "Gentlemen, we didn't just clean the plant, we cleaned our mindset." We clapped, exhausted yet deeply proud. Someone murmured, "Next shutdown, we'll do it again!"

The Abhiyaan helped us learn that a plant, like a person, shines brightest when cared for consistently. Even weeks later, walking past the spotless preheater floor, I still feel a quiet satisfaction. Every time I pass that spot, I whisper softly, almost instinctively, "Stay clean, my friend, inside and out."

Chapter 15
Brownfield Ballet - The 15-Day Feed Pipe Mission

Every plant has at least one brownfield project that starts as a routine modification and slowly transforms into a full-blown epic. Ours was called "Preheater Feed Pipe Diameter Extension." It was one of my most memorable shutdown jobs. The proposal appeared as a single line in a presentation: "Feed pipe dia to be increased – to improve material flow." There was no alarm on anyone's face when it was presented. No one questioned the feasibility. Increasing a pipe diameter sounded like a small improvement, not a project that would dominate the next two weeks of everyone's life. The logic was simple: better flow, less build-up, smoother operation. So everyone agreed.

The complexity only became visible once the drawings were released.

The scope expanded immediately. The new feed pipe was nearly ten meters long. It required full refractory lining and had to match the existing cyclones at both ends. Bellows were needed to absorb thermal movement. It required cutting through an operating plant floor. On top of that, the pipe centre had to align with the kiln hot centre within a tight tolerance. All of this had to be executed during a 15-day shutdown.

Management's instruction was clear: "Fifteen days only."

Engineering's response was less confident: "Fifteen days only?"

We moved into Pre-shutdown mode immediately. The first task was feed pipe fabrication. The pipe went to the workshop with instructions for continuous work in two shifts. The challenge was achieving correct circularity and dimensional accuracy with thick plates that were already stressed and slightly warped. Fit-up took longer than planned. Every weld distorted the shape slightly, requiring correction. Multiple rounds of welding, grinding, checking and rechecking followed. The workshop team knew that even small dimensional errors would create major problems during installation. There was no margin for casual work.

Once fabrication reached an acceptable stage, the refractory lining began. The refractory team inspected the pipe carefully before starting. Internal lining quality was critical, not only for thermal protection but also for material flow. Improper lining thickness or uneven surfaces would create operational issues later. Formwork was installed inside the pipe. Castable refractory was poured and vibrated carefully to avoid voids. This was not fast work. The pipe weighed several tons and once lined, it would be even heavier. After casting, the curing process started and the pipe was left undisturbed. The area was barricaded and access was restricted. Any damage at this stage would have meant rework and loss of valuable time.

Parallel to fabrication and refractory work, procurement activity intensified. Bellows were critical items with long lead times. Enquiries were sent out marked urgent. Follow-ups became routine. Every day, calls were made to vendors asking for dispatch confirmation. The responses followed a predictable pattern: “Material is ready.” “Dispatch today.” “Truck arrangement in progress.” Experience had taught us not to trust any delivery until the truck physically entered the plant gate. Other items were also tracked: gaskets, fasteners, supports, insulation materials, lifting arrangements. Each delay had the potential to block multiple downstream activities. Procurement meetings became daily events. The focus was not cost or negotiation; it was availability and timing. At the same time, contracts were issued for scaffolding, cutting, welding and civil work. Safety documentation was prepared. Method statements were reviewed. Risk assessments were written and revised. The project file grew rapidly, thicker than the pipe drawings themselves.

While physical work continued, the engineering team repeatedly walked the site. Floor markings were made. Clearances were checked. Interferences were identified and discussed. The team visualized every step of the shutdown sequence. The biggest concern was alignment with the kiln hot centre. This was not something that could be corrected later. Once installed, any misalignment would affect long-term operation. The reference points were confirmed. Survey instruments were checked. The alignment plan was discussed multiple times.

As the shutdown date approached, discussions increasingly revolved around the bar chart. Activities were color-coded. Dependencies were debated. Float was reduced to zero. Any slip in one activity threatened multiple others. Every review ended with the same conclusion: "If bellows arrive on time, we're okay." Despite all preparations, there was an underlying tension. PRE-shutdown work gives a sense of progress, but it also hides risks. Many critical activities could only happen once the plant stopped. Until then, everything felt provisional.

On the evening before shutdown, the plant was still running normally. Material flowed through the existing feed pipe. Equipment sounded unchanged. To anyone outside the project team, it was just another operating day. For those involved, it felt like standing at the edge of a long stretch of work with no pauses built in. The next fifteen days would not be measured in hours but in activities completed and problems solved. The new feed pipe sat in the workshop, fully fabricated and lined, waiting. Drawings were reviewed one last time. Phone calls were made to confirm manpower availability. Safety permits were prepared in advance. Everything that could be controlled had been controlled. What remained was execution. The shutdown was about to begin.

At the scheduled time, the kiln was stopped. Fans slowed. Conveyors emptied. Within minutes, the plant shifted from a running system to a worksite. The silence never lasts long. As soon as the equipment stopped, people moved in. Helmets appeared everywhere. What had been a hot, moving process a few hours earlier became a dense, shared construction zone. The feed pipe area filled up quickly. Multiple teams arrived almost simultaneously: scaffolding, cutting, civil, mechanical, safety. Everyone had a job to do and everyone needed access to the same space. This is where brownfield shutdowns immediately test coordination.

Scaffolding teams moved fast. Within hours, a complex network of scaffolds began to rise around the feed pipe area, wrapping itself around existing structures. By afternoon, we had scaffolding everywhere. Some of it was useful. Some of it blocked access. Some of it blocked other scaffolding. Every team had a reason. Mechanical wanted access from one side. Civil wanted access from below. Refractory wanted clearance that conflicted with both. By evening, parts of the scaffolding that had been erected in the morning were dismantled again because they blocked the next activity. This is normal during shutdowns. Scaffolding is never "done." It is adjusted, modified and reworked continuously. The only real mistake is assuming the first version will be final.

One of the earliest critical activities was floor cutting. The new feed pipe required cutting through an existing RCC floor that had been poured decades earlier. As cutting began, sparks flew and progress slowed. Reinforcement bars appeared exactly where no one wanted them. The cutter struggled. Noise echoed through the structure. Dust filled the air despite suppression efforts. Cutting took longer than planned, but by evening, the opening was finally complete.

As soon as the floor opening was complete, the safety team arrived.

"Sir, floor opening hazard."

"Yes."

"Barricade it."

We did. Barricading in shutdown conditions is not just tape and signboards. It is ropes, nets, toe boards, warning boards and repeated instructions to people who are tired and focused on their own tasks. The barricade was adjusted several times as access needs changed. The safety team stayed close to ensure it didn't go wrong. And we were grateful.

With scaffolding reasonably stable and the floor opening ready, dismantling of the existing feed pipe started. Bolts that had not moved in years resisted removal. Heat was applied and impact wrenches were used. Some bolts snapped and the team responded in unison. That was expected. Each removed section revealed more buildup, more wear and more evidence of why the modification was needed in the first place. The old pipe had done its job, but it was ready to retire. By the end of Day 2, dismantling was largely complete.

By Day 3, the focus shifted to the most sensitive part of the entire job: alignment. The requirement was clear. The new feed pipe centreline had to align with the kiln hot centre within ±10 mm. We brought in the theodolite and tapes. Reference points were marked. Lines were drawn and redrawn. Three engineers stood around the setup, each with a different interpretation.

One said, "This reference is correct."

Another said, "No, the offset is from the other beam."

The third said nothing but looked unconvinced.

The Head of Process arrived on site. "Are you sure about this alignment?"

"Yes sir, we've checked."

"How many times?"

"Three."

"Check again. If this goes wrong, we'll have problems for years."

For two days, alignment was checked repeatedly. Survey readings were revalidated. Reference points were cross-verified with drawings. No one wanted to be the person who said "it's fine" too early.

By the next day, the project entered the phase where drawings were no longer useful and the decisions were taken by the field itself. The new feed pipe was ready to be shifted from the workshop. Rigging plans were reviewed again. Lifting points were checked. The crane operator was briefed carefully; this was not a routine lift. The pipe was long, heavy, refractory-lined and unforgiving. Any sudden movement could crack the lining or distort the shell. The lift began slowly. Spotters were positioned at multiple levels. As the pipe moved into position, clearances shrank rapidly. What looked adequate on drawings felt tight in reality. The pipe passed existing beams with only a few centimetres to spare. Once the pipe was roughly in place, temporary supports were installed. No one rushed to bolt anything permanently. This was still an alignment exercise. Small adjustments were made using jacks and packers. Each adjustment affected two other reference points. After every movement, readings were taken again. This cycle repeated for hours. The process department remained involved. They didn't interfere, but they watched closely. Alignment errors at this stage would not cause immediate failure, but they would create long-term operational instability. Everyone understood that.

The next challenge was matching the feed pipe with the cyclone inlet and outlet flanges. The top flange aligned reasonably well. Bolt holes lined up with minor persuasion. The bottom flange did not. Measurements showed an offset of nearly 8 mm. That number immediately changed the mood. Eight millimeters is small in civil work. In process equipment alignment, it is enough to cause long-term trouble. We measured again. The offset remained.

Options were discussed; cutting and rewelding the flange, slotting bolt holes, introducing forced alignment. Each option had consequences. Cutting and rewelding meant time loss and risk to refractory. Slotting holes raised quality concerns. Forced alignment risked stress on connected equipment. While engineers debated, an old foreman who had been watching quietly spoke up. "Sir, shift the cyclone by one kick." There was a pause. He didn't mean redesign. He meant a controlled mechanical adjustment using a hammer at the base support. This is the kind of suggestion that comes with field experience and no amount of theoretical planning can ever offer. It was discussed briefly and permission was given. One measured, controlled strike was applied. The flange moved. Measurements were taken again. The offset vanished.

Throughout these days, one concern remained unresolved: bellows delivery. Every day, procurement was asked the same question. Every day, the answer changed slightly. "Truck loaded." "Truck delayed." "Truck crossed state border." By Day 7, the bellows became the single critical item holding us up. Without them, final bolting and flexibility checks could not proceed. Then, finally, the call came. "Sir, vehicle reached gate." The truck arrived dusty, covered in polythene and travel marks from multiple states. I might as well have been standing there with a diya thali, performing the truck's aarti. The bellows were unloaded carefully. They were inspected immediately.

With alignment stable and bellows on site, final positioning resumed. Permanent supports were adjusted. Bolting began cautiously, following a defined sequence to avoid pulling the pipe out of alignment. Each set of bolts was tightened gradually. After every major tightening stage, alignment was rechecked. Minor shifts were corrected immediately. This slow approach consumed time, but it prevented rework. By the end of Day 7, the feed pipe was installed, cyclone matching was complete, bellows were positioned and secured and alignment remained within tolerance. The system looked complete, but it was not finished. The project had crossed its most technically sensitive phase.

The major mechanical installation was complete, but the project was far from over. In shutdown work, finishing activities often consume more time and energy than installation itself. This phase tested coordination, patience and endurance more than technical skill. The immediate priority was floor restoration. The floor cut created earlier now had to be restored. The civil team arrived with reinforcement bars, shuttering plates and one load of confidence. "Sir, we'll finish by evening." Our collective experience suggested otherwise.

Steel reinforcement was fixed first. Shuttering was installed carefully to avoid gaps around the pipe. Space was limited and access was awkward due to scaffolding and nearby equipment. Concrete pouring took place in stages to ensure proper compaction around the pipe. By evening, the shuttering was still in place. "Sir, we are giving extra curing time for long life." I replied, "If you delay more, we all need extra curing time in hospital." The concrete was finally cast properly and left to cure.

By Day 11, the area resembled a jungle gym. People moved vertically more than horizontally. Communication became harder. Movement slowed. At this point, we finally declared "scaffold curfew." No new scaffolding would be erected without written approval otherwise we'd end up building the Eiffel Tower by mistake.

By now, everyone was running on adrenaline and tea. Shift schedules blurred. People forgot what day it was. Despite fatigue, there was no loss of focus. Everyone understood the importance of finishing cleanly. A large bar chart was displayed in the control room. It became the reference point for every discussion. Completed activities were marked, while delays were highlighted. The project had entered its final phase. Most of the heavy work was complete, but confidence was still fragile. The system looked ready, but it had not yet proven itself. In shutdown work, this gap between "looks complete" and "is complete" is where anxiety peaks. Everyone knows that if something goes wrong now, there is very little time left to fix it.

The first priority was the final alignment check. Even though alignment had already been verified multiple times, no one trusted earlier readings anymore. Too many activities had happened since then. Bolting, civil concreting, scaffold removal, insulation work, any of these could introduce a small shift. The theodolite was brought back once again. Reference points were cleaned, re-marked and verified. Measurements were taken slowly and carefully. This time, there was less discussion and fewer opinions. By now, everyone understood the geometry and the sensitivities involved. The numbers came in within tolerance. We checked again, just to be sure. The results were consistent. For the first time since shutdown began, no one insisted on another round. We had reached the point where further checking would only create doubt rather than improve accuracy. The alignment was formally signed off.

After alignment, we conducted a complete system walkdown. This is one of the most critical but often underestimated steps before restart. Every bolt was visually checked. Bellows were inspected for correct orientation and free movement. Supports were verified to ensure they were carrying load as intended and not introducing stress. Clearances around the pipe were checked again, especially near hot surfaces and moving structures. Insulation was inspected for gaps or loose sections. Temporary supports were identified and removed. The safety team conducted their own independent walkdown and then repeated it jointly with engineering. Floor barricades were removed only after the concrete had cured adequately and the area was declared safe for normal movement. Floor markings were repainted and warning signs were adjusted to reflect operational conditions rather than shutdown hazards. By the end of Day 14, the area no longer looked like a shutdown site but like part of the plant again. That visual normalcy helped calm nerves a bit.

Day 15 arrived early. Restart days always feel longer than others, regardless of how many shutdowns you have handled. People arrived before their shifts officially began. The control room was fully staffed. Process engineers took their positions. Maintenance teams stayed close to the feed pipe area. Electrical and instrumentation teams remained on standby. Communication channels were tested once more. Radios were checked. Phone batteries were topped up. Before initiating start-up, confirmations were taken discipline by discipline.

When the kiln was prepared to receive feed and material flow was initiated through the new feed pipe, there was a brief pause. It lasted only a few seconds, but it felt much longer. Everyone watched the readings closely. Temperatures stabilized. No abnormal vibration was detected. No unexpected noises emerged from the structure. The system behaved as it should. Material flowed smoothly. The control room and the field echoed with applause. Helmets were knocked together in quick congratulatory taps. People shook hands, then skipped straight to hugs, grease and dust forgotten. A fitter laughed loudly and slapped the nearest engineer on the back. Someone raised both arms and shouted, "Its working!" The kiln received the feed pipe like an old friend.

A few weeks after the shutdown, when the plant had settled back into its familiar rhythm and the feed pipe had become just another line on a P&ID, I found myself reading How Big Things Get Done by Bent

Flyvbjerg. What Flyvbjerg described in academic language, we had lived in steel, dust and sweat. Our feed pipe diameter extension was not a megaproject. It didn't involve billions of dollars or international consortia. But in its own way, it was a perfect case study of the same human and organizational dynamics that shape much larger undertakings. The scale was smaller, but the psychology was identical.

The first lesson that stood out was the planning fallacy. We genuinely believed we could finish the job in fifteen days. And technically, we did. But that achievement needs context. We didn't succeed because the plan was accurate. We succeeded because we quietly overcompensated for its optimism. What looked like a fifteen-day plan on paper was executed with the intensity of thirty. People worked longer hours, took fewer breaks and absorbed more stress than any bar chart could capture. In reality, we had planned like it was a five-day job and executed it like a crisis operation stretched over fifteen days. The timeline was met not because it was realistic, but because the team stretched itself to fit the plan, not the other way around. Flyvbjerg's warning about optimism bias felt less like theory and more like a mirror.

Closely linked to that was the absence of reference class forecasting. We had relied heavily on internal confidence and PowerPoint timelines rather than on historical shutdown data. If we had seriously compared this project to similar brownfield modifications done earlier, especially those involving hot alignment, refractory-lined equipment and live plant interfaces, we would have predicted more friction and fewer clean transitions. Instead, we treated it as a fresh problem, assuming that this time things would somehow go smoother. They didn't. The lesson was simple and slightly uncomfortable: experience exists for a reason and ignoring it doesn't make you faster, only more stressed. Next time, the reference won't be an ideal schedule; it will be a real shutdown that went wrong and what it took to fix it.

One of the strongest validations of Flyvbjerg's thinking came from the role of momentum. At no point did the project move forward because of a single big achievement. There was no dramatic breakthrough that suddenly made everything easy. Progress came from small, almost unremarkable closures. One weld completed on time. One alignment approved without rework. One safety clearance signed without argument. Each of these wins was minor on its own, but together they created forward motion. Momentum, once established, became self-reinforcing. People stopped asking whether the job would finish and started asking what was next on the list. Even exhaustion felt manageable when there was visible progress at the end of a shift. The moment momentum slowed, anxiety increased. That connection became impossible to ignore.

Another insight that resonated deeply was modularity. Without consciously framing it that way, we had prefabricated as much as possible before shutdown. The feed pipe was fully fabricated and refractory-lined in advance. Supports were prepared. Hardware was arranged ahead of time. This reduced the amount of complex work required during the shutdown window itself. Flyvbjerg describes this as "design once, repeat often," and while we weren't repeating a standard design, we were isolating complexity away from the most time-critical phase. The fewer unknowns we left for shutdown execution, the more predictable the work became. Every prefabricated element was one less decision to make under pressure.

Then there was the psychology of scale, a concept that made me laugh because of how accurately it described our experience. On paper, this was a small project. No one would call a feed pipe diameter extension a megaproject. But under compressed timelines, high visibility and continuous monitoring, it felt enormous. Sleep deprivation amplified every issue. Minor misalignments felt catastrophic. Small delays triggered outsized reactions. The project didn't become large because of its scope; it became large because of the way it consumed attention and emotional energy. Flyvbjerg's point was clear: scale is not just physical or financial. It is psychological. And in that sense, our feed pipe was a megaproject for fifteen days straight.

Looking back, the most important lesson had little to do with steel, alignment or equipment. It was about stress. Or more precisely, about the source of stress. The shutdown taught us that stress does not come from workload; it comes from uncertainty. People can handle long hours and hard work when they know what they are doing, why they are doing it and when it will end. What drains energy is ambiguity. Each unanswered question multiplies anxiety far more than physical effort ever could. The turning point came when uncertainty was replaced with clarity. Once every activity was clearly defined, every bar on the chart owned by a specific person and every dependency openly discussed, anxiety began to transform into action. The work didn't reduce, but the noise in people's heads did. Humour played an equally important role. We joked about delays. We laughed at minor mistakes once they were corrected. Someone always had a sarcastic comment ready when things got tense. That humour kept frustration from turning into conflict. It reminded everyone that the problem was the work, not the people. In a dusty preheater environment filled with noise and fatigue, laughter always created breathing space. Discipline was the other half of the equation. People showed up when they said they would. Tasks were closed properly. Temporary fixes were avoided. Shortcuts were resisted, even when time pressure encouraged them. That discipline didn't come from fear of review meetings; it came from a collective understanding that any compromise now would return as a bigger problem later.

In the end, the feed pipe extension did exactly what it was supposed to do. It increased diameter. It improved flow. It reduced operational issues. But its real impact was less tangible and far more lasting. It increased our collective confidence. It reminded the team that even under unrealistic timelines and imperfect planning, disciplined execution can still deliver results. It reinforced the idea that complex problems don't require heroic individuals; they require aligned teams. In the world of cement manufacturing, where projects are often judged only by output and availability, this shutdown left behind a shared memory of competence under pressure.

Chapter 16
Out of Syllabus

"Out of syllabus" is the first socially acceptable escape route we learn. During student life whenever a difficult question appeared in an exam, someone inevitably whispered, "This is out of syllabus." The phrase somehow carried instant relief. It shifted blame away from preparation and places it on unfairness. Teachers sometimes reinforced it too. "This won't come in exams," they say, unintentionally teaching students a dangerous lesson that learning is limited by what questions appears in exams. By the time students graduate, "out of syllabus" becomes muscle memory. Then it enters professional life under new names. In departments, it shows up as "not in our scope." In meetings, it appears as "this belongs to another function." In plants, it sounds like "maintenance issue," "process problem," or "vendor responsibility." It is the same mind-set with different phrasing. In manufacturing, this reflex also spreads quickly. Departments draw invisible borders. Mechanical stops at mechanical. Electrical stops at electrical. Process looks away from maintenance. Everyone stays safely within syllabus. Theoretically it all sounds very efficient but in practical situations it creates gaps where problems settle in very comfortably. This is where organizations start paying a hidden cost.

Ironically, the same people who use these phrases often feel overworked and undervalued. They do exactly what is expected and wonder why growth feels stalled. The answer hides in plain sight. Every meaningful opportunity in professional life lives just outside the syllabus. None of this appears in job descriptions. But organizations reward those who step into discomfort. These individuals become problem solvers instead of task executors. They gain context, not just expertise. Over time, they become indispensable.

I had already learned one uncomfortable truth about plants: inefficiency survives because people learn to live with it. What starts as a temporary compromise slowly hardens into tradition and tradition, in industrial systems, is far harder to dismantle than any piece of machinery.

The meeting room was unremarkable. Rectangular table. Whiteboard with half-erased formulas. The familiar smell of over-brewed. Process engineers filled most of the seats. Operations sat quietly, waiting to agree with whoever sounded most confident. I was there as a mechanical representative. So somewhere during my share of speaking, I said, “Let’s reduce SHC.” The silence that followed was quite dramatic. Finally, someone cleared his throat and said carefully, “That’s… not really in your scope. SHC is process.” He wasn’t wrong. In cement plants, SHC exists firmly inside the process domain. I smiled, partly out of politeness, partly because I already knew this conversation would not end cleanly. It rarely does when you question the comfortable boundaries people are already in.

Specific Heat Consumption or SHC, is deceptively simple. It is the amount of heat required to produce one kilogram of clinker. On paper, it's a ratio. In reality, SHC tells you how much energy you're wasting, how disciplined your system really is and how many inefficiencies you've chosen to tolerate. Higher SHC means more fuel burned than necessary. More fuel means higher cost, higher emissions. More stress on kilns. And eventually more scrutiny from auditors. Our number sat stubbornly around 875 kcal per kilogram. It had been there for years. Theoretical benchmarks lived comfortably below 750. The gap was obscene. But familiarity has a way of dulling outrage. Someone leaned back and raised an eyebrow, "Good luck getting that down. Our kiln's been like that since the Nokia era."

Challenge accepted.

I decided to treat SHC not as a process KPI but as a plant-wide symptom. Instead of asking how to tweak fuel chemistry, I asked where heat was escaping. The plant stopped looking like a machine and started looking like a crime scene. False air was everywhere. It entered through cracked expansion joints and through gaskets that had outlived their replacement cycle by several shutdowns. It entered through flanges tightened just enough to pass inspection but loose enough to whisper hot air into the surroundings. False air does not produce clinker. It does not assist combustion. It contributes nothing. But it requires full heating. It's like the freeloading cousin who shows up at your barbecue and eats all the paneer.

Cyclones were next. One cyclone, in particular, had quietly surrendered. Separation efficiency was poor. Meal fell where it shouldn't. Heat exchange suffered. The clinker line staff spoke of it fondly and called it "Old Faithful." I saw something else; a heat sinkhole that swallowed fuel while returning very little value. The calciner told a similar story. Calcination numbers hovered around 85% on good days and dipped dangerously low on others. That meant the kiln was doing work that should have been handled earlier in the system. Kilns are not forgiving machines. Asking them to compensate for upstream laziness is like asking your old uncle to run a 10K marathon after skipping breakfast. Then there was the pneumatic seal inlet. Designed to isolate the kiln system from atmosphere, it had instead developed an open relationship with it. Leakage caused pressure instability, which caused control issues, which caused fuel inefficiency. Everyone knew it leaked. Nobody owned the consequence.

I began building the heat balance sheet like a detective strings yarn across a murder board. Every input was accounted for: coal, petcoke, alternative fuels, primary air, secondary air, tertiary air and all the uninvited guests sneaking in through negligence. Every output was traced: sensible heat in clinker, heat in exhaust gases, radiation losses, dust losses, moisture losses and the infamous "miscellaneous," which usually means losses we stopped trying to explain. When the calculations settled, the result was uncomfortable. Nearly 120 kcal per kilogram was being lost to false air and systemic inefficiencies. It was not because of bad technology but due to out-dated equipment and neglected fundamentals. That number changed the air in the room. Eyebrows that had once been sceptical were now worried. I was still not supposed to touch process. And I didn't. I tuned the system around it. That distinction mattered more than it seemed.

So we started leak audits standing near ducts, flanges, expansion joints. Feeling where hot air escaped where it had no business being. Cyclone replacement was pushed through. Vendors were convinced to work weekends. Resistance was managed with persistence and food. Samosas, in my experience, solve more interdepartmental conflicts than escalation emails ever will. Calciner fuel mix was optimized carefully. AFR ratios were adjusted. Slowly, calcination numbers climbed back to where they belonged. The pneumatic seal inlet was resealed with surgical precision. None of this involved capital-heavy upgrades. No new burners. No fancy instrumentation. Just sealing, alignment, tuning and something rarer than budget: attention to detail.

Two weeks later, we sat in the same meeting room. placed the updated heat balance on the table and waited.

"SHC is now trending at 765 kcal per kilogram," I said. "That's a reduction of 110."

At our production rate of 5000 TPD, the math translated into over 5 crore rupees saved annually in fuel costs alone. The room went quiet again. But this time, it was a different silence. Someone dropped a pen. Another person finally said, "But… this wasn't even your area."

Exactly.

When the dust settled and the numbers stabilized, what stayed with me was not the satisfaction of having reduced SHC, nor the quiet pride of watching fuel bills drop. What stayed was the shift in understanding. The SHC exercise was an example of how to think about plants, problems and responsibility itself. The first lesson was deceptively simple: SHC isn't a process problem. It's everyone's problem. For years, it was subconsciously accepted that certain numbers belonged to certain departments. It was a neat division, logical on paper and completely misaligned with reality. Once I saw SHC as a shared outcome rather than a departmental KPI, the plant revealed itself differently. Every loose flange became a fuel issue. Every poorly sealed inspection door became an emissions issue. Every inefficient cyclone stopped being "process equipment" and started being a mechanical, operational and cultural concern all at once. Ownership, I realized, was not about titles. It was about proximity to loss. That realization led naturally to the second lesson: heat doesn't care about org charts. In meetings org charts make sense. They define authority, reporting lines and accountability. On the shop floor, heat ignores all of that. It escapes wherever resistance is lowest. It flows wherever discipline is weakest. I had seen this pattern before, but the SHC exercise made it undeniable. The biggest losses were not caused by dramatic failures. They were caused by small, tolerated gaps that fell between ownership zones. That led to the third, perhaps most humbling insight: every leak, every inefficiency, every lazy cyclone adds up. Plants rarely collapse because of one catastrophic error. One kilocalorie here, five there. A small air ingress today, a slightly worn refractory tomorrow. Individually, each loss feels insignificant. Collectively, they become a permanent tax on performance. Over time, those losses don't just waste energy, they lower expectations. The danger of that mindset is subtle. When inefficiency becomes familiar, it becomes invisible. Engineers stop seeing leaks as problems and start seeing them as characteristics of the plant. That is when improvement stalls. The SHC work reminded me that efficiency is not lost in dramatic events. It is lost in the quiet moments when no one asks, "Why is this still like this?" Another important lesson emerged from what we didn't do: we didn't introduce new technology. There were no fancy burners, no exotic fuels, no expensive automation packages. What we used instead was awareness. Better inspections instead of better presentations. Better conversations instead of better excuses. That was perhaps the most reassuring outcome of all. In an industry obsessed with capital projects and technological upgrades, it was comforting and slightly unsettling, to realize how much value still sits untapped in fundamentals.

This experience also changed how I thought about questioning. Better questions matter more than better answers. For years, I had been trained to provide answers. To fix, restore, stabilize. SHC forced me to ask questions instead. Where is the heat going? Why does this seal leak? Why has this cyclone been allowed to run like this? Why do we accept this loss as normal? Those questions were uncomfortable because they challenged assumptions people had grown comfortable with. But discomfort, I learned, is often the entry point to improvement. There was also a quieter, personal realization embedded in all of this. Much of what limits performance in plants is not lack of knowledge, but fear. Fear of crossing boundaries, fear of appearing ignorant, fear of being told "this is not your area." The phrase "out of syllabus" is rarely about capability. It is about permission. And permission, in many cases, is something engineers wait for far too long. That is why, when someone now says, "That's out of syllabus," I smile. Not because I want to provoke, but because I recognize the opportunity hiding inside the statement. Out of syllabus is where learning actually begins. It is where engineers stop being function-specific and start becoming system thinkers. It is where responsibility expands beyond job descriptions and into stewardship.

The formulas we used were simple. Almost embarrassingly so. Specific Heat Consumption was nothing more than total heat input divided by clinker produced. The heat balance was basic accounting; heat in equals heat out, plus losses. There was no advanced mathematics involved. The intelligence lay not in the equations, but in the discipline of applying them honestly. The most important rule that emerged from the entire exercise was equally straightforward: find losses, quantify them, plug them, rebalance and repeat. Hence, there was no finish line but only continuous attention.

Chapter 17
The Broken Rod, The Beating Heart and Two Vital Numbers

The Raw Mill rarely gets the credit it deserves. People talk about cement as if it is born fully formed at the dispatch gate, stacked neatly on trucks. They admire silos, kilns and packing plants, the visible ends of the process. But the real transformation happens much earlier, hidden behind thick steel casings and layers of dust, where stone is reduced to powder and chemistry takes over. The Raw Mill stood there every day like a quiet titan. Hour after hour, it crushed limestone and additives into raw meal with a consistency that bred complacency. When something works long enough, people stop seeing it. Reliability, paradoxically, makes equipment invisible. At that time, the mill was enjoying one of its best runs in recent memory. More than five hundred hours had passed without a single interruption. Operators spoke of it casually, "It's running fine," the way people talk about their heartbeat, unaware of its importance until it falters. Preventive checklists were ticked, vibration levels monitored, hydraulic pressures logged. Everything sat comfortably within limits.

Then came that one Tuesday afternoon. The control room was calm in that peculiar mid-shift way when urgency temporarily loosens its grip. Screens glowed softly. Trend lines moved predictably. Someone poured tea, balancing the cup carefully near the console like a practiced ritual. Outside, the mill hummed with its usual low authority, grinding stone without complaint. Suddenly, the sound that followed did not belong to routine.

CLANGG!

BA-DOOM!

A jolt shivered through the floor. It was violent, metallic, unmistakable. For a fraction of a second, there was confusion—was it external? A vehicle? A dropped component? Then the screens told the truth. Grinding pressure collapsed. Hydraulic readings plunged. The raw meal feed flat-lined. The mill had gone silent in the most unnatural way possible. One of the pull rods had snapped. This was not a minor component. It was a 150-millimetre-thick steel pull rod, one of the longest and strongest mechanical elements in the mill. Its job was brutally simple and unforgiving: transmit hydraulic force to push the grinding roller down onto the table. No pull rod meant no grinding pressure. No grinding pressure meant no raw meal. And without raw meal, the kiln would starve.

For a second, no one spoke. And then everything turned into a chaos. Phones rang. Radios crackled. Managers rushed. Maintenance crews were summoned. Updates flew between sections, each one more urgent than the last. In the control room, voices overlapped as people tried to narrate a problem. And in the middle of it all stood Ravi, the operations head. He was calmly staring at the screen, absorbing the data, already running scenarios in his head.

The mill was opened. Inspections confirmed the obvious. The pull rod lay useless, no longer capable of transferring force. The housing was intact. The hydraulics was alive. But the mechanical heart that connected the two had failed. That was the moment the clock started ticking. The MTTR clock.

MTTR or Mean Time to Repair is a deceptively innocent phrase. It sounds clinical. But behind those four letters lie sweat, judgement and fatigue. MTTR is effort compressed into visible hours. In theory, the formula is simple.

$$\text{MTTR} = \frac{\text{Downtime (in hours)}}{\text{Number of failures}}$$

In this case, Downtime = 32 hours; Failure count = 1

So, MTTR = 32 hours

But, those 32 hours were never just a number on a downtime report. They were a dense block of effort, judgment and controlled exhaustion. Hours filled with decisions that could not be rushed and actions that could not be undone once taken. What looks like a single line item in a logbook expands, on the shop floor, into a sequence of heavy, deliberate work where every step carries consequence.

It began with the flower nut. Massive, unyielding, secured by M48 bolts tightened to between four and five thousand Newton-metres of torque, it did not surrender easily. This was not the kind of fastening loosened with impatience. Each bolt needed calculated force, torque multipliers, synchronized effort and time. Tools strained. Metal protested. The work moved forward millimetre by millimetre, with pauses not for rest, but for alignment and reassessment. Rushing here would have meant damaged threads, distorted components or worse, injury. Once the housing was opened, the damaged pull rod revealed itself fully. Extraction was its own challenge. The rod was heavy, awkward and misaligned by the failure itself. It resisted removal, as though reluctant to admit it had failed. Careful rigging, controlled movement and steady hands finally freed it from the assembly. With no replacement available, the broken rod became the only option. It was cut down precisely at the fracture point. The decision was irreversible. Once shortened, there would be no going back. The next step required patience more than strength: re-threading the rod manually. This was slow, meticulous work, demanding precision and consistency. Each thread had to be clean, true and capable of carrying load. Any error here would simply postpone the next failure.

Reinstallation followed, now with a rod shorter than originally designed. The solution lay not in forcing geometry, but in understanding the system. Hydraulic stroke calculations were revisited. Pressures and travel limits were carefully adjusted so the system could compensate for the reduced length without overstressing other components. This was engineering judgment in its purest form, balancing mechanical reality with operational necessity. The housing was reassembled piece by piece. Alignments were checked, loosened, corrected and checked again. Hydraulic pressures were ramped up slowly, deliberately, watched with a level of attention that only comes after a failure. Nothing was assumed. Nothing was skipped. There was no spare part waiting in stores. No vendor on standby. No shortcut hidden in procedure. Only experience, teamwork and patience carried the plant through those hours. That is what those thirty-two hours truly contained.

When the mill finally came back online, the immediate crisis dissolved into relief. But relief in a plant never lasts long. It simply makes room for the next question. Once the noise of breakdown fades, numbers begin to speak. And the number that quietly waited its turn was MTBF. Mean Time Between Failures. If MTTR tells you how fast you recover, MTBF tells you how often you are allowed to relax. It is the measure of peace between storms. The distance between breakdowns. The breathing space a plant earns through good design, disciplined operation and respectful maintenance. It is also the number people pay the least attention to until something breaks.

$$\text{MTBF} = \frac{\text{Total Uptime (in hours)}}{\text{Number of failures}}$$

In this case, Uptime before failure = 506 hours; Failure count = 1

So, MTBF = 506 hours. That means, on average, this pull rod lasted 506 hours before giving up.

Five hundred hours is not a brief span. It invites comfort to settle in, turns preventive inspections into routine rituals and allows early warning signs to dissolve into background noise. In that quiet familiarity, a component can accumulate fatigue unnoticed, without anyone stopping to question whether it is nearing its limit.

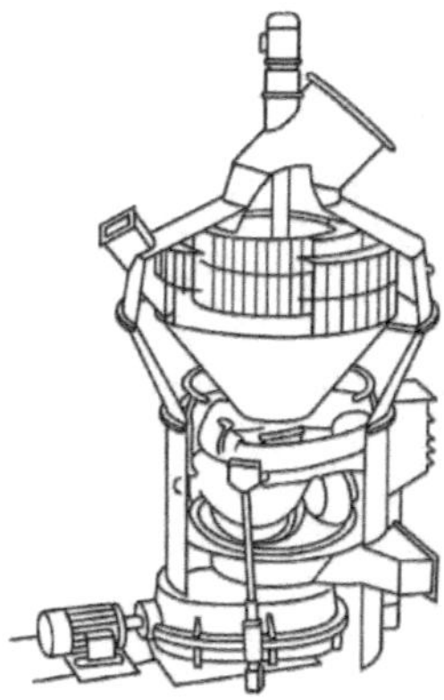

As maintenance teams reviewed the incident, a subtle realization emerged. The rod had done its job. It had survived hundreds of hours under brutal compressive forces. It had endured vibration, load fluctuations and hydraulic cycling. In that sense, the MTBF was not a sign of poor design. It was a sign of honest fatigue. The failure was not catastrophic neglect. It was structural inevitability meeting operational reality. And yet, that did not absolve the system.

As discussions unfolded after the failure, the plant was forced to confront a truth it had previously treated as academic: MTBF and MTTR do not exist in isolation. They are not competing metrics, nor are they interchangeable indicators of performance. They are complementary truths for a plant. While MTBF measures endurance, MTTR measures response. Until that moment, the plant had taken comfort in the numbers. A 506-hour MTBF appeared respectable by any conventional standard. It suggested that the component had delivered a long, uninterrupted service life. It had endured repeated load cycles, thermal expansion and contraction, alignment tolerances and the unavoidable variability of real operating conditions. From a reliability perspective, the pull rod had behaved exactly as designed. It had not failed prematurely. It had not displayed chronic instability. It had earned trust. When the pull rod finally failed, the plant discovered that endurance without preparedness is mere inefficiency.

In textbooks and reliability models, MTBF and MTTR are treated as separate parameters. MTBF feeds reliability curves, failure distributions and life-cycle predictions. MTTR appears in availability equations, maintenance optimization models and resource planning exercises. They are calculated independently, discussed independently and often optimized independently. Plants do not experience them that way. On the shop floor, MTBF and MTTR are tightly coupled, whether organizations acknowledge it or not. The moment a failure occurs, the theoretical separation collapses. In this case, the 506-hour MTBF was completely overshadowed by a 32-hour MTTR. 32 hours is not a maintenance inconvenience. It is an operational disruption. It is lost production, cascading schedule adjustments, crew fatigue and management escalation. It is a reminder that reliability metrics lose meaning when recovery capability lags behind failure inevitability. This exposed a common but dangerous assumption embedded in many maintenance strategies that a long MTBF reduces the urgency of preparedness. A long MTBF is valuable only under one condition: the plant must be equipped, logistically, procedurally and technically, to absorb the failure when it arrives. That means availability of spares, readiness of tools and deployment of skill beyond a single expertise. Without these, MTBF is a misleading comfort metric rather than a resilience indicator. Similarly, MTTR is often celebrated in isolation. Plants take pride in rapid recoveries, heroic maintenance efforts and compressed downtime windows. A short MTTR looks impressive on dashboards and review slides. It signals competence, urgency and technical capability. But MTTR has a hidden dependency. A short MTTR is impressive only if failures do not arrive too frequently. If failures are common, a fast recovery becomes a treadmill. Crews remain in perpetual fire-fighting mode. In such scenarios, a low MTTR masks a deeper reliability problem. The plant appears agile, but it is chronically unstable. True operational maturity lies in balancing both metrics, not optimizing one at the expense of the other. The pull rod failure forced the plant to internalize this balance. The component had demonstrated acceptable endurance.

And so the Raw Mill, rearmed with a shortened but mighty pull rod, got back to feeding the kiln. The lifeline of cement production flowed again. The rollers descended with a familiar hydraulic hiss. Grinding pressure climbed steadily. Limestone once again surrendered to force and friction. The sound returned, the low, steady growl that meant the plant's heartbeat had resumed. Downstream systems adjusted automatically, as if nothing had happened. Ravi watched the trend lines for a long moment before nodding. Manish pressed the final confirmation. The mill was officially back. Thirty-two hours after failure, production flowed again.

What the incident ultimately revealed was something deeper than maintenance strategy or reliability metrics. It revealed how plants actually learn. A failure interrupts complacency. It forces attention. It compresses time and strips away assumptions. And if handled thoughtfully, it leaves behind wisdom passed on from teams to teams. This breakdown did exactly that. The Raw Mill returned to being invisible again, as reliable machines often do. Days passed. Weeks followed. Production targets were met. The kiln downstream never missed a beat. On the surface, the plant moved on.

But during inspections, during planning meetings, during casual conversations on the floor, those two numbers resurfaced. MTTR. MTBF. They had become more than metrics. They had become questions such as "How fast can we recover?" or "How long can we run?" Those questions now lived in the plant's collective thinking. The broken rod had failed under load, but the plant's response had revealed its character. Machines break. That is inevitable. What matters is whether the organization learns faster than the equipment fails. As the notice board near the mill slowly filled with updates and reminders, two numbers remained pinned there longer than most.

MTTR = 32 hours.

MTBF = 506 hours.

Because in the end, plants are not defined by how rarely they fail, but by how clearly they understand failure: how long they can run, how fast they can recover and what it costs when they don't.

There was another side to this incident that was unveiling in my mental floor. When the pull rod failed and the absence of a spare became clear, my first reaction was immediate and instinctive. *No spare meant no solution.* It felt rational at the time. We did not have a spare, how were we supposed revive a fully-damaged pull rod back to life! My attention narrowed. My thinking became transactional limited to who could supply the spare, how fast, and at what cost. Every path I examined led outward. I recognized the pattern only later. Under pressure, my mind had defaulted to threat management. Instead of understanding the system, I was trying to escape the situation. That mental posture consumed energy without producing insight.

But once I stopped trying to solve the problem and started observing how I was responding to it, the solution was right in front of my eyes. Once my emotions stabilized, a subdued form of creative engineering surfaced almost automatically. I stopped seeing the pull rod as a missing object and started seeing it as part of a mechanical relationship. The idea to shorten the pull rod and compensate through adjustment was a simple solution enough. That moment reshaped my understanding of problem-solving under stress.

I now think of the mind the way I think of physical systems. Overloaded systems trip sooner or later. Mental immunity works the same way. It is not built by avoiding pressure but by meeting it repeatedly and learning how to regulate one's response. I also realized that mental immunity is never an individual trait alone. It emerges collectively. Once I steadied myself, the environment changed. This experience also altered how I interpret uncertainty. I no longer treat it as a signal to act immediately. I treat it as a signal to slow down mentally. That discipline of counterintuitive in high-pressure manufacturing environments has proven repeatedly valuable. Just as physical immunity strengthens through exposure, mental immunity strengthens through crises.

Chapter 18
PR Panic, Inventory Illusions & Budget Battles

Let me walk you through simple finance management in a manufacturing unit. At its core, finance in manufacturing exists to answer three basic questions: What do we need to run the plant? How much will it cost? And how do we control that cost without hurting operations?

Everything starts with the budget. It estimates how much money the plant will spend and where that money will go. In manufacturing, budgets are typically divided into heads such as maintenance, spares, power, consumables, manpower, and services. The budget sets boundaries and priorities. Once the budget is approved, actual spending begins. This is where PR, or Purchase Requisition, comes in. A PR is a formal request raised by the department when something is required, such as spares, services, tools or materials. It is the starting point of any purchase. A PR does not mean money has already been spent; it simply signals intent. After a PR is raised, it moves through checks, viz. technical approval, budget availability and management authorization. Once approved, procurement converts it into a purchase order and the material eventually reaches the plant.

Now comes a critical concept: inventory. It refers to materials stored in the plant. Spares, consumables, raw materials, lubricants, and sometimes even finished goods. While inventory feels like safety, it comes at a cost. This is called inventory expense or inventory carrying cost. Inventory expense includes several hidden elements: money blocked in unused stock, storage space and handling, risk of damage, rust or expiry, obsolescence when equipment changes and so on. In simple terms, every spare sitting idle on a shelf is money that could have been used elsewhere. This is why finance teams often push for lower inventory, while operations push for higher availability. Good manufacturing management balances both.

Now that we are solid on the basics, let me tell you about one Tuesday morning. Bright sunny cheerful weather. The tea had the right balance of ginger and sugar. My inbox was unusually calm. Any experienced plant engineer will tell you: this combination is dangerous. It usually means chaos is warming up backstage. Right on cue, Harish from the planning cell stormed to my cubicle. In his hand was a thick, three-page SAP printout, folded and refolded so many times it looked like it had already survived an audit. Dropping into the chair opposite me without asking, "you need to explain this. Please." That "please" carried panic. I took the paper. Bearings. Filters. Motors. Ducting sheets. Couplings. Fasteners. Page after page. At the top, the number screamed in bold confidence:

₹2.3 crore - PRs raised this month (Inventory)

Harish leaned forward. "Do you realise what this looks like? Finance is going to tear us apart in the monthly cost meeting." I scanned the list again and smiled. "We didn't buy a second plant," I said calmly. "This is routine stuff." He didn't smile back. "But SAP is showing it under Inventory," he insisted. "Inventory! They'll say maintenance has lost control. Again." I put the paper down. "Relax. This is where 90% of engineers and at least 50% of finance teams get confused. Your PR is not the villain here." He frowned. "Then why does it feel like one?" "Because," I said, standing up and reaching for a marker, "you're looking at the magician's hat, not the trick."

We moved into the maintenance war room, a space that had seen more arguments than solutions over the years. I wiped a corner of the whiteboard clean and drew three vertical columns.

PR | PO | Consumption

"This," I said, tapping the first column, "is where panic begins."

Harish crossed his arms. "PRs mean money."

"No," I corrected him. "PRs mean intent."

I drew a small kitchen under the PR column.

"PR is like telling the kitchen what groceries you might need this week."

I moved to the second column. "PO is when you actually place the order with the grocery store."

Then the third. “Consumption is when you eat the food.”

I turned back to him. “Inventory is only what’s still sitting on the shelf.”

He stared at the board for a few seconds.

“So… if a bearing was issued for the raw mill last week…”

“It’s already eaten,” I said. “It’s gone. It’s an expense. It has hit your revenue budget. It is no longer inventory, no matter how dramatic the SAP report looks.”

Harish’s eyebrows rose slightly. “Then why does SAP keep screaming inventory rising?”

“Because,” I said, “SAP reports show data but don’t explain behaviour.”

I opened my laptop and pulled out two real PRs from the system. The first was twelve hydraulic hoses for an upcoming shutdown. The second looked similar on paper but felt heavier. A special coupling for a kiln fan after a sudden breakdown. “Both raised by maintenance,” I said. “Both approved. Both sitting in SAP.”

Harish nodded. “Exactly.”

“But financially,” I continued, “they’re not twins. They’re distant cousins.”

I pointed at the first PR. “Routine expense. Planned maintenance. Wear and tear. Expected. Budgeted.”

Then the second. "One-time expense. Failure-driven. Emergency spend. This one spikes the graph and gives finance a headache."

"The problem," I said, "is that SAP doesn't emotionally differentiate. It lists both with the same font, the same seriousness, the same judgment."

Harish sighed. "So every breakdown PR looks like bad planning?"

"Exactly. And every routine PR looks like overspending."

Then I drew a big rectangle on the board and labelled it "STORE."

"Think of inventory as this box," I said. "If something is inside it, it's inventory. The moment it leaves, issued, installed, consumed, it becomes an expense."

Inside the box, I listed:

- Insurance spares
- Emergency motors
- Fasteners stocked in bins
- Filters bought for future PMs

Outside the box:

- A V-belt used during a breakdown
- Lubricants topped up during PM
- A bearing that failed and got replaced

Harish leaned back. "So half of what finance calls inventory… isn't actually inventory?"

"Yes," I said. "Because we raise more POs than we close. Because some planners think stocking 10 of everything makes them safe. And because no one wants to cancel a PR once raised."

He chuckled. "That explains a lot of shouting."

"Here's the uncomfortable truth," I said. "Inventory doesn't rise because engineers are reckless. It rises because engineers are afraid."

Afraid of breakdowns. Afraid of long lead times. Afraid of being asked, 'Why didn't you plan?'

"So they raise PRs early," I continued. "Then they forget to cancel them. Or the item becomes unnecessary. Or the shutdown scope changes."

"And no one cancels PRs," Harish added slowly.

"Because cancelling feels like admitting you were wrong," I said. "And engineers hate that more than audits."

We both laughed.

"But finance only sees the number," he said.

"Exactly. They don't see the story behind it."

Every plant has the same ritual. Costs go up. Someone pulls an SAP report. Filters by department. Points at maintenance. And questions arise like "Why are you raising ₹2 crore worth of PRs every month?" The room goes silent. What that number doesn't show is:

- Items raised for future stock
- Replenishment of already consumed spares
- PRs still under approval
- PRs that will never convert to POs

Until, we track PR raised vs PR consumed vs PR remaining, confusion will remain permanent.

Harish looked at the paper again, then at the board.

"So PRs aren't evil," he said finally.

"No," I replied. "They're just misunderstood."

He smiled. "I owe inventory an apology."

The real damage of PR panic doesn't happen in stores. It happens in conference rooms. Every month, without fail, the same ritual unfolds. A projector hums. A spreadsheet appears. Someone from finance clears their throat. "Inventory has gone up again." All eyes slowly drift toward maintenance. The number on the screen looks monstrous, crores stacked neatly in rows. What the slide doesn't show is timing. A PR raised today may not convert to a PO for weeks. A PO issued today may not deliver for months. An item delivered today may sit untouched in stores until the next shutdown. And the item consumed today may have been raised as a PR three months ago. But SAP doesn't narrate these timelines. It compresses months of activity into a single line item and calls it "current month impact." That's how illusions are born. I once watched a senior manager slam his pen on the table and say, "If inventory is rising, maintenance is not planning." No one corrected him. The tragedy is that once a PR is raised, it gains moral weight. It starts appearing in dashboards and audit trails. It becomes visible. And in organisations, visibility often gets confused with guilt. That's why PRs become punching bags. They're easy to print. And they don't argue back.

There is another cost no SAP report captures: the cost of hesitation. I've seen plants delay PRs because they were scared of "numbers looking bad." The result? Breakdowns get prolonged. Temporary fixes multiply. Emergency purchases bypass planning. Costs rise anyway. All the way making the situation messier. Ironically, the fear of raising PRs often creates the very budget overruns people are trying to avoid. Inventory discipline is not about raising fewer PRs. It's about raising better PRs. Everything else is theatre.

"What's the solution then?" Harish asked me later that afternoon, as we stood near the stores window watching material being issued.

"The solution," I said, "is boring. That's why nobody builds it."

He waited.

"You separate PRs into three buckets," I continued.

- Routine consumption PRs
- One-time breakdown PRs
- Stock-building PRs

Then you track three things:

- PR value raised
- PR value converted to PO
- Material actually consumed

Only the third one is real spend.

“Everything else,” I said, “is just intent and preparation.”

Harish nodded slowly. “That would shut down half the arguments.”

“Yes,” I replied. “Which is exactly why it won’t happen easily.”

One of the strangest behaviours in plants is this: engineers would rather defend an unnecessary PR than cancel it. Canceling feels like failure. So PRs stay alive, like ghosts in the system. Over time, these ghosts inflate inventory reports and feed the illusion of overspending. But cancelling a PR should not be taken as incompetence. It’s maturity. This is what no one understands fully. The more years I spent in plants, the clearer it became: a fearful organisation stocks more, a confident one stocks smarter and a confused one stocks randomly. You can walk into a store and tell the culture of a plant within fifteen minutes. Neatly labelled bins, updated ledgers and aging reviews mean clarity. Inventory is a cultural symptom. When engineers don’t trust systems, they compensate with stock. When managers don’t trust engineers, they compensate with controls. When finance doesn’t trust operations, they compensate with numbers. Each layer adds friction. The store absorbs it silently.

Here's what I wish every engineer knew and every finance manager truly understood. Don't confuse inventory with expenses. Inventory is what's in stores. Expenses are what left it. The ability to distinguish between the two has operational consequences. Inventory ties up capital, yet it also prevents downtime. Expense releases capital into action, yet it also reflects irreversible consumption. Treating inventory as expense only creates unnecessary anxiety. A PR is not an invoice. It's only a request. A PR reflects recognition of a potential requirement. It captures foresight, concern or planning. It does not represent money spent, material received or consumption incurred. Of course large numbers can provoke emotional reactions because they appear final. However a PR initiates a review cycle. It invites scrutiny, prioritization and refinement. Treating a PR like an invoice collapses that process prematurely. Everything issued from store hits your revenue budget, unless you're building new assets. Material issued from stores for maintenance, replacement or repair impacts the revenue budget. This outcome reflects accounting structure, not judgment. The system records restoration of functionality as operating expense. Only material contributing to creation or enhancement of assets flows into capital accounting. Understanding this distinction eliminates confusion. When engineers accept this logic and finance recognizes operational necessity, budget conversations stabilize. One-time repairs should be tracked separately from routine PM jobs. Routine preventive maintenance reflects baseline cost of reliability but failures reflect structural weaknesses. Combining both inside a single cost bucket does not make sense. Separation of the two enables intelligent decisions rather than reactive justification. And finally, don't let SAP reports dictate your understanding. Understand the system first and then read the numbers. SAP records transactions faithfully. But it does not interpret context. Reading reports without understanding process produces false certainty. The next time someone storms in waving a ₹2 crore PR report, don't panic. Smile. Pull out a whiteboard. And say, "Let's walk through this, one nut, one bolt, one bearing at a time."

Chapter 19
From A Naive Engineer to A Responsible Leader

When I joined Mega Cement Company as Head of the Department Mechanical I, my designation changed overnight. Though leadership had been taking root in me long before that moment, the promotion marked a milestone. The imminent transformation demanded inner work and sustained self-examination. The role forced an honest review of my past performance. My technical competence had carried me this far. And now, leadership required something deeper from me. It required emotional maturity. It demanded clarity under pressure. It called for the ability to influence my subordinates positively. Earlier, I worked alongside them, shoulder to shoulder. Now, I had to guide them. I had to take decisions that shaped their work, influenced their growth and carried direct consequences for the company. That realization initiated a deliberate one-year leadership development journey for me. Early in my career, I defined leadership through competence, speed and control. Knowledge was of course my strongest currency. Quick problem-solving also seemed like proof of capability. Command over situations felt like strength. Long hours and visible effort appeared sufficient to earn respect. Results seemed destined to translate automatically into leadership. That belief came from technical training and industrial culture since engineering systems had always reward precision and decisiveness. My experience as a leader reshaped that assumption.

I entered the system with confidence in my technical preparation. Engineering had trained me to diagnose, analyse and correct a situation. Machines followed straightforward logic. Known inputs produced predictable outputs. Breakdowns always had recognizable patterns. This familiarity had given me certainty and speed. Dealing with people as a leader introduced a different equation altogether. Humans respond to emotion, safety and intent. Machines remain indifferent to tone but people absorb it. They seek clarity and reassurance. This contrast reshaped my understanding of work the moment I stepped into real responsibility.

The discomforts of leadership arrived sooner than I expected. Managing people older than me demanded a level of maturity my technical education had never prepared me for. Their experience carried weight. In those moments, authority felt very delicate for me to ascertain. Every word required care. In those moments, presence mattered more than instruction and I felt that gap immediately. Resistance also arrived quietly. Questions sounded polite, even respectful, yet something underneath felt unsettled. Timelines slipped without explanation. People agreed quickly, but their commitment felt uncertain. They nodded, took notes and walked away unchanged. Each interaction left me uneasy. I sensed that the system was responding to my words but not aligning with my intent. In those moments, my instinct pushed me toward assertion. Leadership made every step visible. The moment I moved into it, nothing felt private anymore. Decisions that once passed quietly now carried weight. Mistakes that would earlier dissolve into the system now stood exposed. I felt the presence of an audience even in routine choices.

As these experiences accumulated, a distinction became clear to me through my lived moments. Technical intelligence had helped me solve problems. Now I required emotional intelligence that would help me sustain in the system. My engineering training had conditioned me to value correctness, speed and individual contribution. Leadership demanded connection. It demanded an ability to think beyond individual output and toward collective capability. The system required both dimensions. Watching myself closely, I began to recognize a wider pattern. Many capable engineers struggle during leadership transitions. The struggle often roots from emotional unreadiness. Responsibility expands faster than self-regulation. Authority arrives before influence. Expectations rise before confidence stabilizes. I saw that unreadiness in myself. Under pressure, my impatience surfaced. Curiosity gave way to defensiveness and I spoke when I needed to listen. I reached for control where trust should have existed.

Over time, I realized that safety sat at the centre of everything. People worked differently when they felt secure. Their effort became more sincere. Their engagement became more consistent. But security did not come from reassurance alone. It grew through fairness in decisions, consistency in behaviour and clarity of intent. In fact, intent seemed to matter more than explanation. I noticed that people evaluated my decisions less by their technical merit and more by what they believed my intent to be. Even a correct decision struggled when intent felt unclear. Transparency changed that. When I explained why, rather than just what, trust strengthened. This realization turned my focus inward. I began regulating my tone, especially during pressure. I slowed my pace when urgency tempted haste. I practiced restraint instead of reaction. I created space for people to respond rather than filling silence with instruction. I acknowledged uncertainty instead of masking it. I stayed steady even when discomfort surfaced. These choices required effort. But they also created stability.

I had seen all of it from other side of the table. But on this side, I got a whole different perspective. The system responded in ways I had not anticipated. Technical readiness had opened the door for me. Emotional readiness kept it open. This phase revealed a truth I could no longer ignore. Leadership demands emotional preparedness alongside technical competence. Systems weaken when either remains neglected. Growth accelerates when both mature together. Entering the system required more than skill. It required awareness, restraint and most importantly good intent. Thus, emotional training became the missing curriculum in my journey. Through that learning, my leadership began to take shape as a way of being.

When I look back at the early days of my engineering career, what strikes me most is how ordinary the suffering felt at the time. None of it arrived labelled as learning. It all arrived as chaos. As disruption. As days that began with confidence and ended in exhaustion. In hindsight, those moments formed a curriculum far more rigorous than any formal training I ever received. At the time, I believed I was simply surviving. Breakdowns occurred without warning. Systems failed at the worst possible moments. Each failure felt personal, as though it questioned my competence. I remember standing in front of equipment that refused to cooperate, knowing that production depended on decisions I had to make quickly and with incomplete information. There were no manuals for those moments. Shutdowns had intensified everything. Margin for error was next to none. Every delay echoed loudly. Every decision felt irreversible. I had learned quickly that speed alone did not solve problems. Rushed decisions often created more damage than delayed understanding. Those shutdowns trained my judgment. The lack of spares had added another layer of stress. I had to wrack my brain again and again for a tinge of creativity that could solve the situation without spending a load on new spares. I learned to work with constraints instead of waiting for ideal conditions. That scarcity had sharpened my thinking. It taught me to prioritize, to assess risk realistically and to understand the true cost of every choice. The only constant during those days was the feeling of exhaustion. Many a night had stretched longer than the working day. My mind replayed decisions, conversations and outcomes repeatedly. Those nights eventually made me more patient than a monk. Each crisis had trained a different muscle. Uncertainty trained judgment. I learned to distinguish between what I knew, what I assumed and what I needed to verify. I learned to make decisions without waiting for perfect information. I learned that hesitation carried its own cost. Failure trained humility. Mistakes revealed gaps that success often hides. They taught me to listen more carefully and to acknowledge my and the system's limitations. At no point did all this feel like growth. It felt like struggle. It felt like being overwhelmed. It felt like constant inadequacy. Growth, while happening, felt indistinguishable from stress. There were no markers of progress. Looking back, I see that each challenge built capacity incrementally. None of them alone transformed me. Together, they reshaped how I responded to the chaos.

The turning point of my engineering career happened when I finally understood my place in the system. For a long time, I saw myself as a cog in a vast machine; working hard, rotating fast, trying to prove my strength. I believed that if I performed better, I would matter more. I measured my worth by how indispensable I appeared. But beneath all that effort was an uncomfortable truth I had not fully acknowledged. I was infinitesimally small. Capable, yes. Sincere, certainly.

But replaceable. If one cog failed, the machinery would adjust. That realization made me work harder every day. The real shift in my mind-set began when my role subtly changed from being a cog to becoming a switch. As a switch, my value depended on how thoughtfully I enabled flow. Its functioning depended on how well I served it, not how loudly I asserted myself within it. That distinction changed everything.

Serving the system meant that I release an old habit; the need to be right. For years, being right had felt like strength. It shielded my credibility. It justified my decisions. It gave me confidence in uncertain environments. Letting go of that felt like stepping into vulnerability. Choosing what was right for the system required patience and the willingness to absorb discomfort without immediately resolving it. Ego had to loosen its grip and allow responsibility to grow. Earlier, decisions often revolved around how they reflected on me. Gradually, they began revolving around how they affected stability, continuity and trust. I stopped asking whether a decision demonstrated competence. I started asking whether it strengthened the system. This shift did not reduce pressure. It redistributed it inward, where it could be managed with intent rather than reaction. Speed had once been my greatest ally. Quick responses had earned me appreciation. Every engineer can vouch that rapid problem-solving created visibility. But over time, I saw how speed often masked deeper instability. Fast decisions delivered short-term relief but left behind unresolved tension. I learned to slow down. Stability was the new metric. I needed to evaluate decisions by their ability to endure stress rather than their ability to impress in the moment. Authority also changed meaning. Earlier, authority felt like leverage which allowed me to direct outcomes. Eventually, it felt increasingly hollow. Direct instructions moved people briefly but credibility moved the system forward. Alignment between words and actions was the only way one could build credibility.

I also realised that leadership is often misunderstood as a solitary pursuit. From the outside, it appears to be about standing at the front. Titles even reinforce this illusion- Head, Manager, Director, Leader. But the truth is no leader succeeds alone. The real measure of leadership is not individual brilliance but the strength and capability of the team that surrounds the leader.

Early in my career, I believed leadership meant having answers. I thought respect was earned by stepping in whenever something went wrong. If a problem arose, I felt compelled to fix it myself. If deadlines were missed, I took the burden personally. If outcomes failed, I assumed responsibility alone. While this approach felt noble, it was deeply flawed. It was exhausting, unsustainable and, most importantly, it quietly weakened the very team I was meant to lead. A leader's role is not to replace the team; it is to enable the team to perform at its best. No matter how skilled or experienced a leader may be, individual capacity is finite. Time, attention, emotional bandwidth and cognitive focus all have limits. A team, however, multiplies capability. Diverse skills allow work to be distributed and decisions to be enriched. Problems get solved faster and more creatively than any single person could manage.

When leaders try to do everything themselves, they become bottlenecks. In contrast, when leaders trust their teams, work flows more freely. There is also the other side of the coin. Leadership can be isolating. The higher one goes, the fewer people speak candidly. This makes teams invaluable not only for execution but also for perspective. But a wise leader does not treat the team as an audience, but as a thinking partner. Encouraging dissent, welcoming alternative views and inviting feedback strengthens decision-making. Teams that feel heard are more engaged and more willing to go the extra mile when it matters.

In moments of uncertainty or crisis, it is often the collective wisdom of the team, not the authority of the leader, that navigates complexity best. Titles evolve and roles change. What remains is the people a leader has shaped. One of the most enduring responsibilities of leadership is developing others. A leader who builds capable, confident and ethical teams leaves a legacy far greater than any individual achievement. When leaders invest in their teams they create future leaders. This requires patience and restraint. Allowing others to lead means accepting slower progress at times and resisting the urge to intervene prematurely. However this discomfort is essential. Teams grow only when they are trusted with real responsibility. A leader who hoards authority limits both the team's growth and their own. Perhaps the most transformative realization I had in leadership is that the team does not exist to serve the leader; the leader exists to serve the team. This does not mean appeasement or absence of authority. It means creating conditions where the team can succeed.

Leadership carries many visible rewards, but it also imposes significant costs. Among them, the most consequential is the quiet erosion of personal and family life in service of professional responsibility. This is not a theoretical observation; it is a lived experience. During my years as an engineer in plant operations, professional demands frequently extended beyond defined working hours. My daughter grew up during this period and much of her early life unfolded while I was physically present elsewhere, most often on the shop floor. I depended heavily on my wife to manage the household, provide stability and carry the emotional weight of daily life. While I was responsible for production continuity and operational reliability, she was responsible for everything else. There were nights spent inside the plant troubleshooting critical breakdowns. Those nights accumulated into months and years. Along the way, I missed weddings, family gatherings and personal milestones; absences justified at the time by urgency and accountability, but irreversible in consequence.

Advancement into a Head of Department role did not reduce this burden; it intensified it. The scope of responsibility expanded from technical systems to people, culture, performance and conflict. Managing machines was finite; managing people was continuous. Decisions followed me beyond the workplace, occupying mental space long after formal hours ended. Leadership, I learned, does not conclude when one leaves the site, it persists through unresolved issues and expectations. From an external perspective, leadership is often perceived as offering greater autonomy and flexibility. There is an assumption that senior roles enable leaders to delegate effectively and reclaim time. In practice, delegation redistributes execution, but not accountability. The leader remains answerable for all outcomes including failure. Authority may grant discretion, but responsibility deepens cognitive and emotional load rather than diminishing it.

What becomes evident over time is that leadership consumes not only time, but sustained attention. Families experience this withdrawal not as absence of effort, but as absence of presence. Over time, this imbalance becomes normalized, turning sacrifice into routine rather than deliberate choice. The risk lies in this normalization. When leaders stop questioning the cost of their availability, they begin to equate endurance with effectiveness. Balance in leadership is not achieved through equal allocation of hours, but through conscious prioritization. It requires recognizing when professional commitment begins to undermine personal foundations and intervening before that depletion becomes permanent. Sustainable leadership depends not on constant sacrifice, but on disciplined boundaries that preserve clarity and long-term effectiveness. Perhaps the most difficult skill a leader must develop is not how to stay longer, but how to step away responsibly, without abandoning either duty or self.

Chapter 20
What Truly Matters to Grow as A Leader

Over the years working in the manufacturing industry, experience has earned me the clarity to write this chapter on what truly matters in becoming and growing into, a leader. This perspective did not come from theory or observation alone, but from years spent inside plants, systems and teams where leadership is tested daily. I offer this chapter not as instruction, but as contribution. Manufacturing has a way of stripping leadership down to its essentials. In this environment, leadership is not defined by ambition or designation, but by behaviour under pressure, decisions made in uncertainty and the ability to build trust across heirarchy. This chapter draws from that lived reality. It is written for engineering graduates stepping into the manufacturing world; those who arrive armed with technical knowledge, confidence in logic and the aspiration to lead someday. Technical skill opens the door, but leadership demands far more. It requires emotional steadiness, ethical clarity, physical endurance and the humility to keep learning long after formal education ends. The experiences shared here reflect the lessons I learnt throughout my career. They highlight what textbooks often overlook: that leadership is built through discipline, presence and intention rather than position. That self-awareness matters as much as competence. That resilience is cultivated through care of the body and clarity of the mind. And that trust multiplies when authority gives way to partnership. If this chapter serves as a compass rather than a manual, it has fulfilled its purpose.

Discomfort is the fuel for growth: Whenever we join a new job, our first instinct is to settle in. We want to understand the system, learn its rhythms, avoid early mistakes and earn quiet acceptance. Comfort, at this stage, feels like progress. Once the anxiety fades and the role begins to feel familiar, we assume growth will follow naturally. We believe stability will make us effective, that ease will sharpen performance and that once we are comfortable, we will finally begin doing our best work. But the moment we truly become comfortable, when the role stops demanding adaptation and starts accommodating us, growth quietly stalls. Comfort creates the illusion of competence without demanding expansion. We repeat what works instead of questioning what could work better.

I learned this not during a crisis, but during a period of apparent stability when everything was working well enough to avoid uncomfortable questions. At the time, our cement portfolio was settled. PPC dominated overwhelmingly. It was familiar, predictable and socially validated. Staying within that structure would have been the most comfortable professional choice available to me. No relationships would be strained. No resistance would surface. No justification would be required. Then PCC entered the conversation as a strategic suggestion. Choosing PCC meant stepping deliberately into discomfort. Not dramatic hardship, but sustained psychological friction. Dealers frowned at the lighter shade. Contractors watched site demonstrations with folded arms, waiting for proof rather than offering trust. Internally, teams hesitated, worried about complaints and reputational exposure. For a long time, there was no visible validation. Months later, PCC started being recommended. Dealers stopped asking why it looked different and started asking for it by name. A similar lesson had surfaced earlier, in a far less glamorous setting. Every morning, the same sentence greeted me: "Sir, only one rake today." It was said with ritual certainty, justified by a mythical fear of DC cost. Accepting it was comfortable. Challenging it was not. Ordering a second rake felt reckless, unnecessary, even irresponsible. It invited confrontation upward and panic downward. But the discomfort exposed something deeper: fear had become policy. Once that fear was confronted and more rakes moved without catastrophe, the system's capacity to handle it expanded. Only in hindsight did those lessons become clear. Today, when work feels too smooth, too unquestioned, too easy, I become alert. Comfort, I have learned, is a warning. Growth is almost always waiting just beyond it.

Confront the weakest skill: For a long time, I believed my greatest strength was also my greatest shield. I was technically sound. I understood system precisely. I could diagnose problems quickly and move toward solutions with confidence. In engineering environments, that competence often earns early credibility. People listen when you are right often enough. For years, I assumed that was sufficient. What I did not recognize early enough was that technical clarity does not automatically translate into human clarity. I began to notice a pattern that unsettled me. Meetings would end with decisions technically aligned, yet emotionally strained. Conversations would conclude without conflict, yet leave behind a residue of unease. I would replay discussions in my head long after they were over because something in the exchange felt incomplete, misread or unnecessarily sharp.

My weakest skill was not knowledge. It was communication. I did not lack vocabulary or confidence. What I lacked was awareness of timing, of tone, of how anxiety leaks into language. I spoke to resolve problems quickly, often mistaking speed for effectiveness. I listened to respond, not to understand. When conversations became uncomfortable, my instinct was either to push harder with logic or retreat into silence. Neither helped.

Instead of avoiding this weakness, I chose to confront it deliberately. The first step was inward. I read books that forced uncomfortable self-examination. Ikigai introduced the idea that purpose is not discovered in grand ambition but cultivated through alignment; between what we do, what we value and how we engage with the world. It subtly reframed my relationship with work. I began to see that much of my restlessness came from chasing external validation rather than internal clarity. The Courage to Be Disliked challenged a belief I had never questioned; that approval was a prerequisite for worth. The book articulated something I had felt but never named; that anxiety often stems from living inside other people's expectations. The idea that freedom comes from taking responsibility for one's own life, rather than managing impressions, was uncomfortable. It also felt true.

Reading, however, was not enough. Insight without practice always remains theoretical. The next step was one my younger self would have found unnecessary, perhaps even embarrassing: I hired a tutor to work on my communication. Those sessions were humbling. I became aware of how often I interrupted just out of urgency. How frequently I anticipated conclusions instead of allowing others to reach them. How my desire to be efficient often translated into conversations that felt transactional rather than collaborative. I began practicing structured conversations. I forced myself to listen fully before responding. I learned to ask clarifying questions instead of defending positions. I practiced responding with intent rather than impulse. Gradually, I became less preoccupied with how I was being perceived and more attentive to what was actually being said.

The most significant change was internal. My mind grew quieter. I was no longer reacting. I was responding. Looking back, confronting my weakest skill reshaped my leadership more profoundly than mastering any technical system ever could. Engineering taught me how things work. Communication taught me how people work, including myself. And that understanding, once acquired, continues to compound quietly, influencing every decision, every conversation, every moment of leadership that followed.

Strengthen the body to calm the mind: Leadership is often described as a cognitive exercise. Over time, however, I came to recognize that leadership is equally physical and emotional. The mind does not operate in isolation. It responds constantly to the state of the body that carries it. A fatigued body subtly destabilizes judgement, while a regulated body creates the conditions for calm, consistent leadership. During periods of sustained pressure, I noticed that mental restlessness increased even when external problems remained manageable. It became evident that mental composure was not solely a function of experience or intellect; it was also strongly influenced by physical state. That realization prompted a simple but deliberate shift: I began integrating cycling and walking into my daily routine. These were not fitness goals or lifestyle statements but functional choices. As the body settled into motion, the mind followed. Cycling, in particular, proved to be an effective regulator. The steady cadence imposed structure in me. Without consciously attempting to solve problems, perspectives reorganized themselves in my mind. Many decisions that felt heavy at a desk became lighter on the road. Walking served a different purpose. It slowed the pace of thought. It created distance from urgency. Issues that seemed immediate in confined spaces appeared more proportional when viewed through sustained, unhurried movement. Over time, these practices became reliable anchors for me. They did not eliminate pressure, but they changed how I processed that pressure.

Parallel to this physical recalibration, I addressed another dimension that leadership often side-lines. For years, certain health issues had remained unattended out of prioritization. Work demands had always justified postponement of doctor consultations. Eventually, it became clear that managing complex systems while ignoring one's own was inefficient. Consulting doctors was not a retreat from responsibility; it was an extension of it. Health is not a personal indulgence. It is an operational requirement.

Around the same period, I consciously shifted how I evaluated professional growth. Alongside performance and compensation, I began investing deliberately in skill earning. Each new skill added optionality. Each layer of competence expanded confidence. That confidence, in turn, reduced fear by increasing my capacity to navigate it. Skill earning reframed my relationship with work. Growth became cumulative rather than situational. As my capability increased, anxiety naturally receded. Taken together, these changes reshaped my leadership equilibrium.

Have difficult conversations: One of the most defining moments of this journey unfolded during a meeting with my team. There was nothing extraordinary about the setting. Routine conference room. Familiar face. But as I looked around the room, I saw capable people who worked hard and met targets. But beneath that surface stability laid a deeper concern. Comfort had settled quietly into the culture. So I asked the first question, "What will you do if you lose your job tomorrow?" The room responded with a panicked silence. I had to clarify that it was not a layoff meeting before someone fainted. Once the team regained itself, the question cut through routine thinking and disrupted assumptions that had accumulated over time. Then I asked the second question, "What will you do if you die today?" The atmosphere shifted. The room moved from professional alertness to personal reflection. People turned inward for answers. These questions demanded engagement at a level daily work rarely touches.

I spoke to them with clarity and intent. Employment provides income and short-term stability, but continuity is sustained by relevance. Skills move across roles while adaptability compounds steadily. A role serves the present, but capability secures the future. Career stability rests on what an individual carries forward rather than on the structure that employs them. Markets evolve, systems realign and organizations reorganize as a natural consequence of change. Skills endure through these shifts. Learning strengthens independence and continuous growth expands both confidence and choice. The second question carried equal force. Time moves without negotiation and opportunity favours those who are ready. As I spoke, the same standards applied inward. You know, leadership carries exposure. I told the team what I expected moving forward. Appraisal of salary mattered but appraisal of skills mattered equally. Each person owned their trajectory to which the organization can only provide a platform.

Work towards being partners: My relationship with the team evolved decisively after that meeting. Hierarchy gradually gave way to partnership. Earlier in my career, appreciation often carried an unspoken undertone of control. Recognition acknowledged effort, but reinforced that hierarchy. Authority defined roles and distance preserved order. That approach delivered structure and predictability. It ensured alignment and maintained discipline. It also created boundaries that limited ownership.

In manufacturing, seriousness comes naturally. The environment demands precision and accountability. Machines operate within narrow tolerances. In such settings, leadership often defaults to gravity. Seriousness hardens into rigidity and rigidity restricts connection. That is where humour earns its place as a leadership tool. Humour, used with intent, introduces balance. It softens edges without diluting authority. It creates psychological space in environments that tend to compress it. A well-timed smile or a light remark can dissolve tension faster than a directive ever could. It reminds people that beneath roles and responsibilities, they remain human. I learned that humour functions best when it carries respect. It never targets individuals or trivializes work. Instead, it reframes pressure. During intense shifts or long troubleshooting sessions, a moment of levity often reset the emotional tone of the room. Humour also served as a bridge across hierarchy. A shared laugh erases distance without erasing structure. It allows leaders to remain approachable while maintaining clarity. When people feel at ease, they speak more freely. They raise concerns without hesitation. They admit uncertainty without fear. That openness strengthens the system.

One of the most visible changes came through something deceptively simple: tea breaks. Stepping away from desks and machines erased the invisible lines that hierarchy quietly sustains. During those moments, titles would dissolve. Conversations flowed without agenda. People spoke freely, not as subordinates reporting upward, but as professionals sharing perspectives. A cup of tea created a neutral space where authority softened and trust surfaced naturally.

My understanding of leadership matured through my career. I made a conscious shift in how I engaged with my team. Gratitude and praise became intentional rather than procedural. Appreciation moved beyond acknowledgment and became recognition of effort and initiative. I thanked people clearly and sincerely, without attaching control or hierarchy to the gesture. Partnership also raised standards. When people feel trusted, they protect that trust. Performance improved without pressure. Motivation emerged internally rather than through reinforcement. The most meaningful change was psychological. The team no longer worked for leadership; they worked with it. This transition strengthened leadership rather than softening it. Authority supported by trust carries greater influence than authority maintained through distance.

Treat continuous learning as a discipline: In manufacturing, like any profession, change is the only constant. Systems evolve. Software upgrades. Roles change. Places of posting change. Bosses change. Teams change. Amid all this movement, the single constant that enables survival and eventually growth, is adaptability. In a world that refuses to stand still, adaptability is the most reliable advantage. To thrive in the constantly changing landscape of manufacturing, learning must become a discipline rather than an occasional activity. Learning, however, does not mean accumulating technical facts or collecting certificates alone. It is far broader, more practical and far more human. Learning happens as much on the shop floor as it does in a classroom, as much at a tea stall as it does in a conference room. Every environment carries knowledge. Every person carries experience. The discipline lies in remaining receptive.

One of the earliest lessons manufacturing teaches is humility. A technician who has spent decades around machines often understands failure modes, workarounds and operational realities far better than a newly appointed manager armed with fresh degrees. Experience accumulated over years cannot be replaced by hierarchy or titles. There is no loss of authority in learning from subordinates. On the contrary, it strengthens leadership. When leaders remain open to learning from those around them, respect flows naturally. Knowledge begins to circulate rather than stagnate. The shop floor is a living classroom. It teaches constraint, improvisation and cause-effect relationships more effectively than theory ever could. Conversations during routine tea breaks often reveal operational insights that never surface in formal meetings. Learning to listen, without ego, without preconception, is a powerful leadership skill. Continuous learning begins with curiosity and is sustained by humility.

Alongside experiential learning, technical competence remains essential. Manufacturing evolves rapidly, driven by automation, data and digitization. Technologies that once seemed futuristic now define daily operations. When I joined the cement industry, mobile phones were a luxury item. Communication relied on landlines, handwritten notes and physical presence. Today, mobile devices are as common as a pen in the pocket. Information flows instantly. Decision cycles have compressed. Visibility has expanded. Technology has reshaped how work happens. This transformation reinforces an important truth: relevance decays quickly without renewal. Technical knowledge demands constant updating. Processes improve. Tools change. Best practices evolve. Leaders who remain anchored to what once worked risk falling behind quietly. Continuous learning ensures alignment with the present while preparing for the future.

At a certain stage in my journey, I recognized the need to formalize this learning. Experience had taught me patterns. It had sharpened instinct. But complexity was ever increasing and decisions carried wider implications. To deepen perspective and structure thinking, I enrolled in an MBA program and began completing multiple online courses. These were not academic checkboxes. They were instruments designed to refine judgment, strengthen decision-making and improve people management. The MBA provided structure to my experience. Concepts such as trade-offs, positioning and long-term value creation offered me important frameworks to organize assets and manpower. Online courses complemented this by addressing specific gaps in my knowledge. Each new concept added dimension to my leadership skills.

Continuous learning also changed my relationship with fear. Fear often emerges from uncertainty and limited options. Learning expands options and equips leaders with multiple lenses to interpret situations. With greater understanding comes confidence and grounded assurance. I was no longer running away from fear. I was building a foundation strong enough to stand on. Learning also cultivated patience in me. Concepts absorbed through study encouraged reflection before action. Importantly, all my learning integrated seamlessly with work. It did not sit outside professional life. Concepts found application during meetings, negotiations and reviews. My leadership matured through alignment between knowledge and action. In manufacturing, much like any other field, leadership longevity depends on relevance. Relevance depends on learning. Learning depends on discipline. This discipline needs consistency. A willingness to observe. A readiness to ask questions. An openness to learn from anyone and anywhere. Continuous learning remains one of the most reliable investments a leader can make.

My journey so far resembles the bus ride I once took on my first appointment to factory-crowded, sweaty, restless and moving forward whether I felt ready or not. If I could go back to that ride, standing awkwardly with one hand gripping the overhead rail and the other holding uncertainty, I would tell my younger self to be more patient and far more observant. To watch the people as carefully as the destination. To learn quietly from the processes unfolding around him. To start a conversation with the co-passenger instead of retreating into nervous silence. If I could return to the first night I was called to the plant mid-sleep, heart racing and mind clouded by fear, I would tell myself to slow down internally, to understand that panic is not urgency and urgency is not competence. I would tell him that this moment was teaching an essential skill to think clearly while tired, to act decisively without full information, to stay functional in discomfort. If I could visit myself lying on the operation table for gallstone removal, lights overhead and vulnerability fully exposed, I would tell myself to take care sooner and better, to listen to the body with the same seriousness reserved for equipment alarms, to understand that neglect compounds quietly until it demands attention at the worst possible moment. If I could sit beside the young father watching his child grow between missed dinners and postponed weekends, I would tell him to seek balance earlier, not as a moral ideal but as a structural necessity, because leadership that drains personal life without replenishment eventually weakens both. I would tell him that presence is not measured only in provision and that time, once traded repeatedly, cannot be repurchased later with intention alone. And yet, despite all these things I would say, I would not change the trajectory of my career. I would not soften its edges or rewrite its demands. Because what I am today was shaped not by comfort, but by accumulation of fatigue, responsibility, learning, failure, restraint and persistence. The path did not unfold neatly, nor was it chosen cleanly; in many ways, it chose me. Each uncomfortable moment added a layer of understanding. Each delay sharpened my judgment. Each mistake refined my attention. Looking back now, I no longer see my journey as a collection of disconnected episodes, but as a single, continuous formation. Each experience shaped the next. And the clearest understanding I carry today is this: growth happens in small invisible stances, through repetition, fatigue, responsibility and persistence. Only later, in hindsight, does its shape become visible, when you realize that the journey, crowded, restless and exhausting as it was, built precisely the capacity it kept asking of you.